# How to Get Your Pet Into Show Business

## Captain Arthur J. Haggerty

**HOWELL BOOK HOUSE   NEW YORK**

MAXWELL MACMILLAN CANADA   TORONTO

MAXWELL MACMILLAN INTERNATIONAL   NEW YORK OXFORD SINGAPORE SYDNEY

Howell Book House
Macmillan Publishing Company
866 Third Avenue
New York, NY 10022

Maxwell Macmillan Canada, Inc.
1200 Eglinton Avenue East
Suite 200
Don Mills, Ontario M3C 3N1

Macmillan Publishing Company is part of the Maxwell Communication Group of Companies.

Library of Congress Cataloging-in-Publication Data
Haggerty, Arthur J.
How to get your pet into show business / Arthur J. Haggerty.
p.    cm.
Includes index.
ISBN 0-87605-559-5
1. Animals in the performing arts.   2. Animal training.
I. Title.
PN1590.A54H35   1994
791.8'023—dc20              94-674           CIP

Macmillan books are available at special discounts for bulk purchases for sales promotions, premiums, fund-raising, or educational use. For details, contact:

Special Sales Director
Macmillan Publishing Company
866 Third Avenue
New York, NY 10022

10  9  8  7  6  5  4  3  2  1

Printed in the United States of America

To two people without whom
this book would never have been written:

CAROL LEA BENJAMIN

a great dog trainer and writer, whose suggestions
and encouragement moved
the project forward

*and*

JUDY NELSON

a great writer who worked on this
book with me until her untimely death

*and*

to my teachers, the ones that have always
taught me the most about animals,
the animals themselves:

MUG-Z

owned by Kathy Mills Ahearn, is the
genius of theatrical dogs,
with an amazing repertoire of tricks

*and*

GO-GO BURROUGHS

best known for
appearing opposite Jon Voight
and Sylvia Miles in *Midnight Cowboy*

# Contents

# Preface

This is a book about the handling methods used in show Business. The small "s" and capital "B" are deliberate because it's more business than show. I'm going to teach you the business.

Everything you need to know about getting your pet into show Business/showBiz is in this book: methods, advice, tips, suggestions, tricks and caveats.

In truth, most work is for dogs, with cats a distant second. If you don't have a dog, don't despair. Read on. I'll tell you how to get work for your cat. You don't have a cat? I'll tell you how to handle your bird, your reptile, your fish (yes, fish, too), your tarantula, your horse, crustacean, antelope, koala bear or whoever is your best friend. It is said that there is a commercial for everyone. Even if you have two heads, there is a commercial for you. The same is true of animals. If you have a Kirtland's warbler, there is a commercial for your pet partner. Why should your pet be a waiter its whole life?

You'll see, from the inside, the different areas of showBiz:

- TV commercials

- Print jobs (for animals with fashion models in slick magazines)

- Feature films

- Industrial shows and films

- Fashion shows and runway work

- Stage, from Broadway to local theater groups or, better still, from local theater groups to Broadway.

I even have information on pricing. I'll tell you how much to charge.

I'll show you how to behave on a set. How to promote your pet.

But the real thrill is the glamour, the glitz, the adventure, the razzle-dazzle. Show Business is the stuff dreams are made of. And let's not forget the name-dropping. When I look at the list of people that I have worked with, *I'm* impressed.

Don't think you won't have a chance to hobnob with show-Business personalities because you live in Fargo, North Dakota. You're wrong! Feature films are made all across the United States, in Canada and throughout the rest of the world. Why shouldn't you break a bagel with Bronson? Don't quit after your first job just because Burt Reynolds isn't on the set. He'll be there one of these days. He was for me, twice!

I've always loved animals. I remember in my preteen years attending the prestigious Westminster Kennel Club annual show in New York. I was awed by the presentation and preparation of the wonderful show dogs. I wanted to be a show dog handler myself, an impossible goal for a kid who dragged home every stray, explaining to my mother how it "followed me home." Then I discovered dog training. That was an attainable goal. I worked with as many people as possible and "stole" as many ideas as I could. This was in the years before the onslaught of dog training books, each advocating a new, quick, unique, foolproof method.

When it came time for me to serve in the military I tried to get into the Army K-9 Corps. In retrospect I realize that young soldiers do not have their dreams fulfilled, especially if there is a need for combat troops. In combat, however, the U.S. Army fulfilled something of that dream by letting me go on patrol with a scout dog. That dog, with its early warning of approaching enemy personnel, saved my life and the lives of those on patrol with me. I volunteered to go out on patrol every night with the scout dogs. There weren't many scout dogs available, and very few soldiers had the pleasure of working with them.

I was lucky. I got out of combat alive, with four Purple Hearts. When I returned to peacetime duty I had the chance to participate in off-duty Special Service activities putting on plays. I was a ham. My interest in animals and training continued, and so did my dream of joining the K-9 Corps. Along the way I picked up a commission, and there was no chance of an officer getting such an assignment. Furthermore, it would have violated the military tenet of assigning someone to a job for which he was qualified.

Then serendipity entered the picture when I received one of the most undesirable stateside assignments: Fort Polk, Louisiana. They had a saying that *no one* could get out of Fort Polk until he finished his assignment. It didn't matter to me because I loved the assignment. Then I found out that the Mountain and Cold Weather Training Command at Fort Carson, Colorado, had an undersubscribed course. I knew two things. When I went to ranger school, the cadre raved about this course. They had all taken it. That was reason enough to apply. I knew something else, however. The Army Dog Training Center was at Fort Carson and I wanted to see it.

When I submitted my application, everyone knew that I couldn't get out of Fort Polk, especially if it was to take a two-month course in a winter playland. The difference between Carson and Polk was considered by the military to be greater than that between heaven and hell. But I enjoyed Fort Polk and was fascinated by the wild animals, particularly the feral pigs and the rare dog breed indigenous to the area, the Calahoula hog dog. Everyone at Polk was convinced Haggerty was not going to escape. Then the orders to the course came down. I was getting a temporary reprieve!

When I arrived at Fort Carson I went to the office of the Army Dog Training Center and requested permission to see the training. Why was I interested, the major wanted to know. I gave him a thumbnail sketch of my dog-training experience by way of explanation. He told me to report back to him after seeing the training center. This I did. I exuded enthusiasm. Then out of the blue he asked me how I would like to be assigned there. I was overjoyed and said it was a lifelong dream. He told me what to do. I had to go to post headquarters and report to a colonel up there. The colonel was impressed. I was a desirable commodity at the time: a young infantry second lieutenant with fruit salad on his chest. I was both combat and ranger qualified. They all loved that gung-ho stuff. The colonel disregarded the rule about putting someone in a job he was qualified for.

They would start the paperwork at ADTC up through Fort Carson headquarters to Army Command and then on to the Pentagon. The cumbersome chain of command would have to be followed. I was to initiate my paperwork at company level in Louisiana to battle group to brigade to post headquarters to Army Command and the papers were supposed to meet at the Department of the Army in the Pentagon. On returning to Fort Polk I submitted the paperwork. It never got out of brigade. They kept kicking it back. They were not going to permit me to leave. There is another rule in the army: Keep the paperwork moving. The Fort Carson paperwork didn't stop at the Pentagon. My orders were signed by the secretary of the army, Wilbur M. Brucker. Brucker signed everything. Still another army rule says: Do everything you are told by those above you, especially if he is the secretary of the army. My company commander, First Lieutenant Motsenbacher, called me in, convinced I knew somebody in the Pentagon. He thought that I knew Wilbur M. Brucker. No, I didn't know him, never met the man, but I will be eternally grateful to him.

I left to take charge of the 25th Infantry Scout Dog Platoon. Serendipity. You and your pet must make the most of those fortuitous breaks in *your* showBiz career.

After getting out of the service, I returned to New York to train dogs. Animal agencies began to call on me more and more frequently to handle the "hard" jobs that were beyond them. They weren't hard for me, but they required creativity and imaginative solutions. When asked if I could do a difficult job, no matter how complex, I'd always answer, "Yeah, sure!" Then I'd be asked, "How much?" Once I figure out how to do a job, then I can tell you how much it costs. Read this book and you will learn that, too.

From my perspective there are no negative experiences. You learn from all your experiences. If you're stuck with a lemon, make lemonade. Don't complain because there is no work for your Emperor penguin. Find the tuxedo or ice cream company that will be interested in using your nonflying fowl.

In the course of this book I will tell you about a number of people who achieved success, including a highly paid computer programmer who started his own animal agency, a professional trainer who has the fun and glamour of going into New York City to do commercials and print jobs for added income and the fellow out in the boondocks with a passel of Shetland Sheepdogs who put together his own dog act. I'll tell you their stories, and more.

Some jobs just require an animal to "stay." Appearance or cuteness is often of overriding importance. You may have the only creature capable of doing the job. You will, after reading this book, know the ins and outs of the business and how to whisk past all the competition. You'll learn some common (and uncommon) tricks. You'll learn not only *how* to get your beast buddy into show Business but also how to *keep* him in it. You'll learn that *handling* rather than training is the important skill. You'll learn how the business is structured and who to contact if you want to get Figaro into a dog food commercial. You'll learn who to talk to if you have a problem, and who not to talk to. You'll learn about the ups and downs, the joys and frustrations—and if you find out that this is more work than you want to put up with, then the price of this book is money well spent. You'll know the reasons for *not* going into show Business.

Thomas Alva Edison said, "Genius is one percent inspiration and ninety-nine percent perspiration." In that last word transpose the second and third letters, and drop the "s," change the first "i" to "a," and perspiration becomes preparation. I'll show you a no-sweat way to do the preparation. Who said you can't get there from here? Knowing the route to take reduces the perspiration factor and increases the success factor. Let's start!

# Getting Your Foot
# in the Door

Your very first question will be "How do I get work for my pet?" Believe me, he or she will not be discovered in Schwab's Drug Store. A major factor in your modus operandi is your location. No matter what geographical location you are in, there is a need for your services. Granted, there are advantages and disadvantages to every location. If you are in the middle of Africa there are no theatrical animal agencies, but if someone wants to photograph African wildlife in realistic surroundings, no place is better. Surprisingly enough, *many* African animals have been brought into Africa from the United States because of the dearth of performing animals.

Suppose we want to put you together with the photographer/cinematographer of the production company. In the middle of Africa, how do you get to be known? Well, you could hire a plane and a pilot that does skywriting. Who is going to see it? The Grant's gazelles? It would be different if there was a production company way out in the bush that you were unable to reach. Then the skywriting might work! The idea is to make it work for you. A better idea would be to contact all the great white hunters, the local tourist bureau, or the organization that strives to get film production into a particular country (See Appendix 1).

In my case I was an officer serving with the U.S. Army in Berlin, Germany. One of my assignments was coordinating the use of the Berlin Police Department's K-9 section with the U.S. military's escape and evasion training program. (Berlin during my tour of duty, and for a long time after World War II, was technically an occupied city.) A local film company needed a Dalmatian to play a short but key role in a film they were shooting. They contacted the *Hauptinspektor*, Simmons, who was in charge of the Berlin PD dog section. The police department had no Dalmatians, but the inspector referred them to me. After all, I was an American and a dog trainer. America's preeminence in the film industry assured the Germans that I was the right man for the job. Naturally, when asked, I told them I could do the job, and I did. Being at the right place at the right time helped. Networking (see Chapter 10) with a big *macher* like the inspector helped. The cachet of being an American dog trainer convinced the Germans that they had a big Hollywood dog trainer on their staff. Another factor is that while there are many fine trainers in Germany, they are not set up or geared to do this type of work. Neither was I, but that never stopped me before. They were happy with the work on their film *Schwartzer Kies* (Black Gravel), and I did my first commercial film venture.

Let's get back to your situation. Large metropolitan areas have more competition, but the route to success is well marked, and it's easier to reach your destination. These larger areas have animal agencies that, with a little bit of luck, will sign you up. Give them a call. Tell them what you have and ask them if they would be interested in representing you. If they ask for some pictures, send them along. Follow up with a phone call, on the pretext of seeing if the photos arrived. Don't be a pest but keep pestering them. If they seem interested, ask them if you can bring your animal in to show them what it looks like. This is particularly worthwhile if you have a supertrained animal that you can use to impress the agency. If they want to handle the whole thing over the phone and/or through the mail, go along with them. These people can be unbelievably busy and may not have the time to see your animal. Do not, I repeat, *do not* show them your dog or cat unless it can at least do a sit stay. A high level of training in a dog or cat is an excellent selling point. Cuteness, while of primary interest to the ultimate user, is the second best selling point to the agency. Less "obedience" training is expected of exotic animals, but you *must* be able to handle and control them.

Florida-based Johnny Robb supplied her first animal for a Buick commercial in 1985. She was a natural for the business. She had worked in film and television production and she owned her own horse. She knew how the business worked. How the business works is very important, and this book will teach you that. Johnny's advice is "If you get into that local stuff, especially with cats, it gives you an opportunity to get experience on the set and build a résumé."

Some animal agencies specialize in certain areas of the business: dogs and cats, exotics, big cats, hooved animals, etc. If they do not handle your type of pet, network with them. Who do they know that does handle your animal? They should know about you. Someone, somewhere, sometime will ask them for a recommendation. Network!

While it's easier to get started in large metropolitan areas, it does not mean that you can't get work in the boondocks. Skip Norwood is in the Florida Keys—a pretty remote place. He is a sea captain (he has a master's license), PADI diving instructor, marine biologist, pool shark (he can't get away from those fishes), underwater photographer/cinematographer, former stunt man, actor, and most importantly, production coordinator. He is

CanDo Production Services. If you need a fish or an alligator or a dog, Skip can put it together. He's done five commercials for Omi cigarettes, a Middle Eastern company. He has been in business three years and they keep coming back for his animals. And the Florida Keys are in the boondocks.

In a relatively small town you have more control over your animal's fate as a show Business star, and that is still spelled with a small "s" and a capital "B." I know you are interested in the show, but they are interested in the business. Keep that in mind and handle your precocious pet like a business. In a small, remote town you can cut out some of the middlemen. You are not interested in cutting out the middlemen altogether—you just want more control over your pet's destiny. You don't have to go to an animal agency if there isn't one. *Technically* you are required to have a license from the United States Department of Agriculture (see Appendix 1 for the address) in order to supply animals for entertainment purposes. If you work under the umbrella of an animal agency, you are covered. You can go directly to the production companies, even if there are very few of them. You may decide to go directly to the person at the local business, such as a department store, who's in charge of advertising. The owner of the department store may be the very one handling the advertising. This is a good deal. There is no one stopping you from reaching the one person who makes the final decision. Too many people run interference in large companies and cities, which means there are more people who can turn thumbs down on using your pet. Believe me, if you are turned down at the lowest level, even by the mail clerk, no one higher up will know about you and your wonderful animal.

When you reach Mr. Department Store Owner, have a plan for using your pet in advertising. Give him something specific. "I saw your brilliant full-page ad with the models in tweedy fall fashions. Chuck, my Labrador Retriever, would add a lot to an advertisement like that. It was an outdoor shot, and Chuck is great off leash. There is nothing more outdoorsy and tweedy than a Labrador. We all know that an ad with a dog in it really draws attention." The store owner knows you are on the ball. Not only did you see his ad but you liked it. You know how to make it better. You know his advertising thrust.

Be prepared for at least two backup suggestions in case he doesn't like that one. If you can suggest using Chuck in an ad that, unknown to you, is on the drawing board, you are home free. That is highly unlikely. Offer to look over any ads he has on the drawing board. The ad agency will not be happy, but if you have the store owner's ear, there is not much they can do to stop you. Offer to use Chuck in an in-store presentation to reinforce the ad's message. Offer to do the in-store gratis if you do the ad. Be bold! You will probably have only one shot at talking to him, so make sure you sell him.

Hammer home the advantages of using an animal in the ads. I remember that one woman's magazine I supplied animals for said that their newsstand sales leapt forward when the cover girl held a cute puppy or kitten.

Be ready with your backup advertising plan using animals. There is a true story about two writers who were trying to sell a film idea to a studio head. They were turned down on their original proposal, but they came up with two other ideas. When the alternate ideas were turned down they kept throwing out ideas off the top of their heads. The studio head bought the last idea and ordered a treatment.

"Which idea did he buy?" one partner asked the other after they left.

"I don't know, Murray!" George answered.

"What do you mean you don't know? It was your idea," Murray said.

"I thought it was your idea," George retorted.

"What are we going to do?" Murray wanted to know.

"Write him a treatment! He probably doesn't remember what he okayed anyhow," George rightly concluded.

It's that kind of crazy business, and that's the way things are done in movieland. You only get one trip to the trough, so have your alternate sales pitches ready.

I was training Sugar, a Bichon Frise, for the owner of a small firm who asked me how he could deduct the training costs as a business expense. I told him to use Sugar in his advertising and the training and other dog costs would be deductible. He didn't even have a logo, but he was in the cleaning business, and the Bichon, a sparkling-white dog, was ideally suited as a logo. He claimed a 20 percent increase in business when he started using Sugar. People would come in just to see the dog.

In a large city it would be foolish to walk in to sell the department store owner on using your pet. You probably would not be able to get an appointment. The only possible way to handle this sort of sales pitch is via a personal meeting with the store owner at a friend's house or cocktail party. If you don't have a recommendation and someone laying the groundwork, you will waste your time and conceivably embarrass yourself. Furthermore, the department store is probably part of a multinational, multibillion-dollar corporation. With animal agencies you don't have to do as much legwork. The agency has the contacts and the contracts. The jobs come to them and they assign the right animal. The agency has the necessary U.S. Department of Agriculture license and the right insurance coverage for this type of work, and can give you access to more jobs than you can get yourself. They will probably hire you as a subcontractor or independent contractor, which means that you will have no workman's compensation insurance. Taxes will be your responsibility because the animal agency will not withhold them. You have less control over your destiny in the larger metropolitan areas, but there are more opportunities.

Just because you are in a large metropolitan area does not mean that you can't be out there promoting your pet. The most time-efficient way to make these contacts is through the mail, and the most effective way of getting the job is in person. Use a combination of the two. Approach photographers first. It is easier to get to see them. Mail them your information and follow up on the phone. Make an appointment. Photographers are used to models dropping in. Photographers have a little more latitude in selecting talent, so it isn't necessary to go through an advertising agency. When at the photographer you may be asked for photos. Explain that you do not have any, but casually mention you would be willing to use your dog for test shots. For a test shot the photographer pays the model little or nothing. The model uses these test shots for his/her portfolio. The photographer does the same. This is your chance to get some very high-quality photos while ingratiating yourself with the photographer. If you know what kind of work the photographer does, you can make specific recommendations for test shots that would pique his or her interest. Get in there early for the appointment and you can see the photographer's work on his wall. Think of suggestions before speaking with him. Your purpose is *not* to have test shots done. Your purpose is to show the photographer your pride and joy. Do not hard-sell test shots. Hard-sell your animal. Subtly mention test shots, and if there is a glimmer of interest, go for it!

The quality of photos is important. If you do not have good photographs, go with Polaroids. Creative people, advertising people, and others in this business are geared to seeing the best photography, and if what you have isn't good, you will turn them off. There is a subtle message with Polaroids that says that these are not professional shots but "something I just did for a quick look." It also subconsciously says that these are current, up-to-the-minute shots. When you get some good photos, go for some 8 × 10 glossy photographs that are mass produced. There are specialty houses that do this type of work. Your first hundred should cost you less than sixty cents each. If you can't find anyone in your community, check with those in New York, Chicago, or Los Angeles. This can be handled by mail, but I prefer to walk them into the processor to talk one on one.

Check in with your state or city film commission. It is financed by your tax dollars to attract film and TV production to your area. It is supposed to know all the answers. Give the commission the answers before it is asked the question by a production company. A list of film commissions, members of the Association of Film Commissions International, can be found in Appendix 1. Don't feel guilty telling them about you and your pet. It is their business to know all of this information. You are helping them. In some cases they put out a catalog listing local suppliers, for which they charge a listing fee. Hold off on spending a lot of money until you have a better feel for the business. Remember, it is a business, not a self-aggrandizement project.

A surefire way to get started is with your own animal act. Animal acts are considered an anathema in show business. People love animals, but animal acts just do not appear as headliners in Las Vegas. The popular exception is Siegfried and Roy, which is also a magic act, but magic acts are also an anathema in the business. So sue me! You can make an animal act a success; just be the best, like Siegfried and Roy. There is a whole subculture in show Business known as the party business. This consists of self-contained acts that entertain at parties and other functions. Human actors have survival jobs. Generally actors become waitresses, waiters or cab drivers before they are "discovered." Some of them flex their show Business muscle by going into the party business as jugglers, stand-up comics, magicians, singers, belly dancers, clowns, face painters, card readers and celebrity impersonators. Not only are they able to say that they have been working in the business full time for years, but they are also gaining valuable stage experience.

Another aspect of party business is street entertaining. Just collect a crowd and strut your stuff before passing the hat. This is encouraged in some areas and discouraged in others. Check with local authorities before passing the hat. Street entertainers are honing the skills that they may someday be called on to use. You and your boa constrictor can do the same thing. Put together an animal act and you will be continually working on improving your animal's performance. Should you enter the party business, keep in touch with other performers. They are continually booking friends to work with them. Don't frown at a dog and pony act; it could be the start of something big.

A man went to an agent seeking representation for his act—bird impressions.

"Are you crazy?" shouted the agent. "Vaudeville is dead. Bird impressions! We don't even have the 'Ed Sullivan Show' anymore. Get out of here!"

The man flew out the window.

Cruise ships have a ravenous appetite for varied entertainment. They prefer an act that can be made to appear like different acts with a change of presentation and costume. If your talent enables you to come up with two different acts, they will love you! What could be finer than taking an ocean cruise, living in the lap of luxury and getting paid at the same time? The work is not unduly hard, with one or two performances on each leg of the journey. It may not be the best-paying job in the world, but it makes for a great vacation. You can also try your act out at hospitals and nursing homes. They are always interested in something to entertain their long-time patients.

Setting up an animal agency yourself is an ambitious project, but it can be done. Get as much experience as possible before taking the big plunge. Be prepared to lay out a good amount of cash, particularly for insurance coverage, which is not only expensive but hard to get. A possible stumbling block is stringent governmental regulations, which you'll have to check out. You would be surprised how many people in the business work out of their hats and homes. You do not need plush offices.

Susan Zaretsky, a fine trainer from Walden, New York, established an adjunct to her dog-training business: Party Pups and Clown Around. She would give a children's party dressed as a clown, accompanied by her highly trained household pets. She found that not only did she have a lot of fun, but it also led to other animal-training jobs. Even pig-training jobs.

You can't afford to sit back and wait for everything to come to you. You have to get out and hustle. Contact any animal agencies in the area. Bill Vergis of the prestigious Jungle World in Clewiston, Florida, prefers training the dogs and cats he works with himself, particularly if he has them interacting with his exotics. His specialty is exotic animal work, and he doesn't care for small jobs, which should be where you get your start. He, like others in his category, can use some outside animals. Why not send these people photos and résumés? Call up the ad agencies. Ask questions. Send out your business card. Make a video of your performing pet. Make the rounds. Develop your and your pet's skills. Get your animal out of the unemployment line. Keep pounding on doors. Success is just around the corner.

# II

# What Area of the Business Appeals to You?

"Nobody is worth
what they pay
me."

**Burt Reynolds**

So you want to get your pet into show Business. I know, I know, your pet is prettier and smarter than those animals you see on TV. But do you want to do commercials, movies, stage or what? There are all sorts of ways to get your pet (and you) into show business. What avenue should you take? I'd suggest all of them! Do all of them at once and then choose what suits you best.

Let's start off with an animal act. No, it isn't impossible. Should you have a cat that does dog imitations, you have a built-in act. If you have more than one animal, this is even a better way to go. Las Vegas for the New Year's Eve show? What about opening for Frank? Before you book Vegas or open for Frank, you better get some experience under your belt! Let's start off with freebies such as nursing homes. Ordinarily, nursing homes don't pay, yet you will get experience and a great deal of satisfaction bringing sunshine into the lives of the people living there. It won't look terrific on your résumé, but it will do your heart good. You can book hospitals and nursing homes directly, yourself, by phoning and telling them what you have in mind. If they haven't used animals before, you will have to wait for an answer. Don't be shy. Follow up. Don't load yourself down with jobs, however. Keep at least two weeks between assignments so that you can rework and improve your act. It is also possible to be paid for these jobs, so don't assume there is *never* any pay. Starting out, it is more important to get the work than making money.

If you want assistance in booking hospitals and nursing homes you may find it easier to do it with a group, such as Therapy Dogs International (see Appendix 1). Local humane societies and SPCAs may supply animals for this purpose. The Delta Society certifies animals for pet-assisted therapy. If you have a dog, particularly a purebred dog, check with your local American Kennel Club all-breed club and you may find that they would be eager to have you help them. Explain that it will help them meet the AKC's desire that they do dog-related activities in the community. They are always interested in staying on the good side of the American Kennel Club, and the AKC is interested in educating the public about responsible dog ownership.

Since you *may* not get paid for entertaining in hospitals and nursing homes, you are right in asking, "Where's the Business in show Business?" It shows you are learning! You have to start someplace.

A woman called me and wanted to work handling dogs for film and TV. I asked her what dog-handling experience she had, and the answer was none. Before you can successfully handle animals in front of a camera, you must have animal-handling skills. The woman explained how she loved animals (it is easy to say you love animals—we all do) and I told her she could volunteer to work in an animal shelter. But, she said, volunteer work was not her cup of tea. How could she get into the business? An alternative, I suggested, would be to get an apprentice job in a kennel doing menial work, at low pay, as a stepping-stone to learning dog handling and training. She had no time for this slow step-by-step procedure. Still another alternative was suggested: Take a course to become a dog trainer. It is a definite shortcut for entering the field, particularly at a higher rate of pay. She didn't have the money or time for that. She wanted to start at the top. I told her she was like the parent of a child who has just completed the seventh grade and wants the child to be a brain surgeon. The child just loves brain surgery, would be willing to take a free short course, and then walk into the operating room to perform the first operation. I don't want to be on that operating table!

No business is going to take someone in and pay a higher salary than the other employees earn while giving that person an accelerated, complete course. It wouldn't be fair. That potential employee has not proved him- or herself. The only thing that person has is "love" of animals. That love has not been established, merely stated. It sounds like fun. Pet animals and become a star. There are many people who say they want to become actors. They do not want to be actors, they want to become *stars.* No, not "become." They want to *be* stars. Don't try it. It is hard to become a working actor. An easier entry into the field is to handle showBiz animals, and here you are! An example of one animal handler/trainer who successfully made the transition is Dan Haggerty, the "Grizzly Adams" of TV fame. Dan Haggerty (no relation to the author) was a wild-animal trainer. According to that great animal trainer Frank Inn, Dan was terrific and absolutely fearless with wolves. But it was bears that moved him on to TV stardom.

Often I would bring a dog down for a director to see and the director would ask me if I would like to be in the film because of my unique appearance and perhaps a touch of charisma. I usually agreed, and a friend, April Pollack, said that I was foolish not to join the Screen Actors Guild. I met April when I trained her dog, Lord Jim. This is a good example of networking. I was a ham, and the next time I was asked to appear in a film by director Buzz Kulik, I followed April's advice and sprang into action. The union has a great catch-22. You can't work in a film unless you are in the union, and you can't join the union unless you've worked in a film. April coached me well. I finessed my way into the union. Now I supply myself for films more frequently than animals.

Without owning the well-trained animal(s) to build your career on, how can you enter the field? Why not try getting a job as an assistant to an animal act? It's a tough job to get, but it's a logical step in entering the business. The easiest way is to do it on a part-time basis with your own animal, as many readers of this book will do. There is an ongoing need for a limited number of people to assist in all types of animal exhibitions.

## ★ TELEVISION

There are two general areas in which animals are used in television: advertising and entertainment. Entertainment can be broken down into sitcoms, soaps, movies of the week, episodics, variety, comedy shows, etc. The general rules listed under "Film" apply. Just remember that in episodics or sitcoms there is a better chance of getting recurring work from week to week or even a contract.

Your pet would be perfect for commercials. Smart, beautiful, just what they need for this ad campaign. You even have a great idea for an ad campaign mapped out for that special product. Your Nubian goat can be the spokes-goat for the recycling campaign of a major manufacturer of packaging. You've heard it said that goats eat tin cans (which are made of aluminum). Actually the goats are going after the glue on the back of the paper labeling around the cans, but you know the image. Why not have your Nubian give a pitch for recycling between chomps on the cans? Great idea! Funny! In truth, the chance of selling something like this is, at best, difficult. That is just not the way ideas are developed. If the business is a one-man operation or a small family-run business you have a shot, as I mentioned earlier. But if a major manufacturer has a vice president in charge of advertising, who works with the firm's ad agency, you have a lot of people who can say no on your way to the top person. You have to start at the bottom, and anyone from the office boy up to the president of the ad agency can say no. They know that they can get into trouble saying yes, but not if they say no. People at the ad agency are paid to be creative. They are supposed to come up with ideas. They also have been working on something for the last eleven months that they are trying to sell to the packaging manufacturer. They jealously protect the client from outside influences. It is highly unlikely that your timing will coincide with that millisecond when the ultra-creative ad agency is desperately searching for an idea. If you know the advertiser's president you have entree to the inner circle, with only one person able to say no.

# ★ MODELING

We all know what a model is, and we have seen pictures of animals modeling, or at least being an accoutrement. There are a number of areas of modeling that you can pursue.

## Fashion Shows

Fashion shows are easier to get if you work cheaply enough. Everybody in the rag business is looking for a bargain. Fashion shows are a lot more work than they appear. It is not simply walking down the ramp with a model. The animal must be rehearsed in walking down a high ramp. Even if carried instead of being led on a leash, it must be trained. *Caution!* On runway work I cannot stress the importance of training and conditioning the animal. You always have to worry about the footing for your pet. Unsteady footing will frighten most animals. Runways are well made and solid, for the models' safety if nothing else. It is firm footing. What animals are afraid of is *the edge.* Remember that. You will run into this problem even on a low tabletop or chair that you want your pet to sit or stay on. The animal must also be the *right* one for the job, in appearance as well as temperament.

## Print Jobs

Print jobs need animals. The big advantage of this work is that you can get a photographic record of the job to add to your pet's book. Catalog advertising is generally considered the lower-paying end of modeling. The other end of the spectrum is high-priced fashion shooting. Quality photographers at either end turn out artistic masterpieces, always worthwhile for a book that you will show to prospective clients. They are always looking for the right animal to enhance their photographs. Your black panther would be right on for evening clothes but less than desirable for tweeds/sportswear. In expensive high-end photography the results will have you *kvell*ing for years. If you are outside of the major metropolitan areas, you can present your idea on a print job to local retailers.

Information on editorial work, labeling and point-of-purchase displays is contained in Chapter 9, "The Financial Reward."

## ★ FILM

Film is the longest shot in the business. On the high end, less than 10 percent of the scripts that are written get optioned. One percent get produced. Locating scripts with animals in them can be done. It is not for the fainthearted. You will have to comb the trades for leads. They list films that *might* be produced or are preproduction. You have to be systematic, hard working and willing to pursue every lead. If the film is taken from a book, read the book. Networking is important. If you know a screenwriter, hold her or his hand and have your animal put in the script. Follow that script. It is a long shot but it is a shot. The sure-fire way is to produce the film yourself. That is a case of the tail wagging the dog.

In television animals, primarily dogs, are used in series, usually sitcoms. They will also appear in made-for-television movies, and here is where the film rules apply in television. Your antennae should go up when you hear about a series that will have an animal in it.

## ★ STAGE

There is no money in community theater, but it abounds throughout the country. There is a constant demand for animal actors in community theater. Generally, new plays are not produced. It is the old standards that are most successful, and you should know which ones require animals. Some of these productions will recognize the need for professionally trained animals and wind up paying more money to the animal than to the leading actor. Paul Goldie developed Paul Goldie's Theatrical Animals, Inc., by supplying Sandy to a local production of *Annie.* Even at the most amateur production level, someone has to supply, transport and handle those animals. Why not you? It is a place to start. And then, why not Broadway?

Paul Goldie is a successful computer programmer. He also was a part-time drummer—a musician who knew his way around show Business. He also was a dog owner. Martin Charnin's super-successful play *Annie* is a perennial favorite with all sorts of theater groups. One of these groups contacted Paul to see if they could use his dog. Paul went along with them. He had been bitten by the showBiz bug long before his first *Annie.* He loved it! It was more fun than being a musician. It was more fun than working with computers. Goldie did a smart thing. He went to a trainer for instruction in dog training and handling. He was on his way! He was getting more *Annie*s. He then came to me for additional instruction. Not only for training for *Annie,* his specialty, but for other theatrical work. At this writing he has done over forty *Annie*s, in addition to many other projects.

Stage is the hardest, most demanding end of the business. For time, effort and energy expended, it is the least rewarding financially. You do have the instant reward of hearing the audience applaud, and that makes it worthwhile.

Can you do it? Why not? Others have!

# Some of Those Who Have Made It

"The worst part of success is trying to find someone that is happy for you."

**Bette Midler**

Will you and your animal make it? That depends on both you and your animal. Others have made it. Show Business is tough to break into, but working with animals is a great entry-level position. Some animal trainers started from humble beginnings and reached tremendous success. Some, mentioned here, have made millions. "The business has been very good to me," explains Frank Inn, who maintains that he is "comfortable." Cowboy Joe Phillips manages to play golf every day. How do you measure success? The Rockefellers can't afford to play golf every day. Others have started out in the animal business and progressed to success in other areas. Dan Haggerty, as I said earlier, started out as an animal trainer and wound up a TV star in his own series as "Grizzly Adams." Still others (the majority) will do a few jobs and realize it isn't for them. Worse-case scenario: They have fond memories that they can look back on years later. For a fleeting moment they had their place in the sun or chance in the spotlight. Even film stars are sometimes shooting stars: a momentary flash of success that rapidly fades. Let's hope that you and your pet are the stars—and millionaires—of tomorrow.

## ★ KATHY MILLS AHEARN

All trainers have one great dog in their lives, the one that is so responsive and so easy to train that the trainer looks like a genius. Very often it's their first dog, and they are so successful that they enter the professional dog-training field. When asked about this "first" or "best" dog, they will usually qualify their remark with "I guess" or "I suppose." The really fine trainers realize that they have continually improved over the years, and a later dog, which may do a lot more than the earlier dog, is the result of improved training skills.

Kathy Mills Ahearn is an exceptional trainer. Two decades ago she took my dog trainer's course and finished at the top of the class. She is a natural athlete, quick, intelligent, and inquisitive, with a feel for dogs. Her great dog is Mug-Z. The stray was six months old when Kathy rescued it. Kathy's biggest problem was finding new and different things to teach the super-bright Mug-Z.

Kathy is no different from readers of this book. She knew she had a great dog and she wanted to get Mug-Z into showBiz. She did many of the things mentioned in this book and succeeded. Being in the dog-training business helped, of course, but sound advice was the main reason for her success with Mug-Z. I had the utmost confidence in Kathy and Mug-Z and could always rely on her when the chips were down, even when she wasn't working for me full time.

Mug-Z is a marvelous dog. She knows over fifty tricks, many of them cute, such as going to bed and pulling the covers over herself. Scratching herself on cue might not be as cute, but there are occasional demands for this sort of work in commercials. Mug-Z did a political commercial for the Robert Goodman Agency in Baltimore, in which an actor sitting on a porch disparages the opposing candidate. The actor remarks that if you lie down with dogs you are going to get up with fleas. The actor turns around and Mug-Z, with split-second timing, scratches as the actor says, "See what I mean!" In a Christmas tree commercial, complete with Santa, snow and trees, Mug-Z lifted her leg on one of the Christmas trees—and Mug-Z is a female. Split-second timing is important because of the time constraint of commercials, and Mug-Z certainly had it with her repertoire of tricks. Mug-Z even did a TV commercial for me in which she did break dancing. The tag line for that commercial was "From break dancing to housebreaking, we train your dog right!"

But it hasn't been all commercial work for Mug-Z. She is a soap opera star as well, having done "All My Children" three times. She answered the phone, sat up and begged, picked up items and handed them to the actors and in general performed all sorts of interesting tasks to add zip to the script.

At this writing Mug-Z, the former foundling, is fourteen years old. The years of training given to Mug-Z by Kathy has this old-timer walking with pep to her step. That conditioning, training and exercise have kept Mug-Z young. Yes, she has to take Dilantin for her epilepsy and Lasix for her heart. She is hard of hearing, so the earlier hand-signal training has helped immensely: Hand signals for silent commands on a film set can be used later on as a life-saving tool. Kathy is an excellent trainer, and she was wise enough to realize that as smart as Mug-Z was she might be using "selective hearing." In other words, pretending not to hear so she wouldn't have to do something she didn't want to do. Mug-Z is Kathy Ahearn's great dog. Frank Inn's great dog might surprise you.

# ★ FRANK INN

In the mid-1930s a car came sailing across the highway and smashed into Frank Inn. He was rushed to a hospital in Culver City, California, where he was pronounced dead by Dr. George Ham and sent to the morgue. A group of student morticians were waiting for their instructor to appear. They were learning embalming, and their project lay in front of them—Frank Inn. Thank God, the instructor was late! One observant student determined that Frank was still alive. It was not to be the end of Frank Inn but rather the beginning. If it weren't for that sharp-eyed student there would be no Cleo, no Benji, at least not in the form that we know them.

Frank had an enormous hospital bill staring him in the face, and no hospitalization. A friend, Art Close, took Frank under his roof and started the long nursing process to bring Frank back to health. Frank, confined to a wheelchair, was housebound. Art's son, Bobbie, had a dog that "followed me home." Bobbie's mother tried unsuccessfully to find the owner of the stray, much to the joy of her son. The stray's owner probably knew the dog was in a family way and wanted to avoid the responsibility. Shortly thereafter the stray presented a litter of pups to the family. The dogs were placed, except for Bobbie's favorite. The boy explained to Frank that if Frank told the family he'd like the dog for company the pup could stay. The Closes gave permission, and Frank had company when the family went to work and school.

Both he and the pup learned from one another. Frank's companion, Jeep—named after a dog cartoon character, preceding the fabled American military vehicle by a number of years—managed to take a dump in his room and nearly wound up at the pound. Frank, wheelchair bound, couldn't walk Jeep and had to learn about housebreaking. Fast! The solution was to cut a hole in the door. There were no doggy doors then but the family made one.

Thin slices of sausage were what Frank used to motivate Jeep. One day the paper boy arrived and Jeep put his mouth on the paper. Frank threw a sausage to stop Jeep from slobbering on the paper. The ritual continued every day. Frank knew how to stop Jeep from slobbering on the paper and Jeep learned how to get sausages. The movement of one arm and one leg was all Frank could manage at the time, but Jeep picked up on those cues. They taught one another how to teach Jeep to retrieve and hold the paper. When asked today about food reward, Frank says, "I use whatever is necessary to do what needs to be done." Frank is not a "foodie." He is a trainer.

One day, when Frank was encouraging Jeep to come closer, he reached over the side of his wheelchair. Frank tumbled over and the chair landed on Jeep, who let out a ghostly series of howls. Jeep was pinned under the wheelchair. A neighbor, hearing the howling, came rushing in and righted Frank while releasing Jeep. The neighbor told Frank if he needed any help at all to let him know.

Now Jeep was afraid of the wheelchair. Frank encouraged him to come closer with the ever-present sausage. It was slow work, but Frank had time and was making progress. One day Frank was again leaning over the side of the wheelchair and, again, it nearly tipped over. This time Frank righted himself before falling, but not before Jeep started to bark. Frank learned that he could get Jeep to bark with a wiggling movement of the wheelchair. He could also get the neighbor to come in and help him reach something by getting Jeep to bark. Frank, Jeep and the neighbor were well on their way. They were all learning about training. "Training is nothing more than common sense," explains Frank, "which few people have." He is quick to add, "including politicians."

When Frank was back in one piece, or in a series of semimended pieces, he returned to work at MGM. The people at the studio liked Frank, and knowing of the accident, gave him some light work sweeping up cigarette butts. One day on the set he watched Henry East, the grand old man of film training, handle a dog for a film on the sound stage he was sweeping. Frank spotted the error that East was making in his handling of the dog. The dog was supposed to climb up a flight of stairs, enter a bedroom, jump into bed, crawl under the covers, and stick his head from the other end of the covers and bark. The dog was not working because East put the food reward he was using under the covers. The dog smelled the food, and rather than climbing under the covers, he bit at the blanket where the food was located. Frank told Henry he had a dog that could perform the routine. The skeptical East said, "Oh, yeah. I'd like to see that."

The cast and crew broke for lunch, and Henry continued practicing to get his dog to perform. Frank went and got Jeep. He showed up and repeated his statement to Henry East. Frank took a ball and used it to lure Jeep up the stairs into the bedroom and onto the bed, and gradually he got Jeep further and further under the covers. Frank tricked Jeep into thinking the ball was under the covers and the dog worked his way down under the covers and out the other side. By this time Frank had replaced the rocking, tilting chair with a finger signal, which he gave to Jeep. *Voilà*, Jeep barked!

Henry East was impressed. He offered Frank fifty cents a day and a place to sleep if Frank would come to work for him. Frank explained he was making $29.10 a week. East said that, in addition to the fifty cents, he would give him $5.00 a day for each day at the studio. Frank accepted. East putting a roof over his head was worth money, and what Frank didn't tell East was that his salary was garnisheed because of his hospital bill. After the $15.00 for that was deducted, he netted $11.00 a week after taxes. At fifty cents a day Frank was on his way!

Rennie Renfro, another well-known trainer né prop man, saw Inn working and wanted to know what East was paying him. He told him fifty cents a day, and Renfro offered him a dollar a day. But Frank added he was getting $5.00 a day for studio work. Renfro offered him $7.50 a day for studio work.

Next Frank Weatherwax (the brother of Rudd, who was Lassie's trainer) let Inn watch him work with Toto on *The Wizard of Oz*. The Weatherwax brothers recognized Frank's talent and offered him $5.00 a day and $10.00 a day for studio work. They decided, as insurance against being outbid by another trainer, to raise him to $10.00 a day and $25.00 a day for studio work, an unheard-of sum at that time.

Frank was moving onward and upward. He had the opportunity to work with the greatest of trainers at an ever-increasing salary. Carl Spitz supplied trained dogs to other trainers for film work, and Frank had the chance to use a number of his dogs over the years. "Papa" Spitz looked like the old German trainer that he was. He didn't have long conversations with Frank, but one day when Frank was returning a dog after a day's work on the set, Papa presented him with a bottle of whiskey. The surprised Frank wanted to know why. Carl answered in his German-accented English that the dogs did not charge the water bucket when he returned them. It went without saying that Frank would keep his dogs comfortable and well watered, unlike many other handler/trainers in the business. Frank found a champion in Carl Spitz. The ring came full circle when years later Carl's son, with a couple of partners, took over Frank Inn's animal rental business.

With over a half-century of training movie animals under his belt, Frank is very selective about the jobs he takes. And it is a very large belt that he wears. Frank is a big man physically. He is also a big-hearted man. He is continually financing his private charities to help those less fortunate than himself. For example, he supplies a van, complete with the insurance, to transport the elderly in his church group. Frank is also a big man in animal training. He has trained some of the world's best-known animals, such as Cleo, the Basset Hound, and Arnold, the pig from "Green Acres." Today, his best-known animal is Benji.

If you have an opportunity to watch a *Benji* film, notice the genius in film making. Joe Camp produced a script that, with as few words as possible, tells a complete story. Great for children—and international sales, because it requires a minimum amount of dubbing. Even D. W. Griffith could have taken lessons from Camp on how to put out a silent film with as few title cards as possible. We, however, are interested in the animal work, and it is a sight to behold. Even Joe Camp doesn't realize what a genius he has working for him. Benji is never looking off-camera at the trainer, Frank. He is constantly looking exactly where he should be looking. There is not a false frame in the film.

Frank is training Benji for his next film. Frank's a little older now and has to take things easier. He gets around in an electric golf cart. Frank does table work with Benji. Putting Benji on the table Frank sits in his electric golf cart as he trains. Will Frank handle Benji in his next film? Well, that depends on when they are shooting it and how he feels. Benji will be ready and then Frank has the luxury of making that decision at the last minute. It is ironic that Frank started training dogs in a wheelchair and has reverted back to that device. You can't keep a good man down, and Frank is the best.

# ★ SUSAN ZARETSKY

Susan Zaretsky is a true animal lover. She is also allergic to them! That doesn't keep Susan from working with them, however. Over twenty years ago Susan worked for Matthew Margolis, when the southern California–based dog trainer was located in New York. She gave lessons in the home, a good way for her to work with dogs without aggravating her allergy; her not being in constant contact with the dogs presented less of a problem. Susan had her own dogs, though, so she was never allergy free. Her one great dog was Melissa, a cute stray with a shyness problem. Was it a great dog or great training that salvaged Melissa? Even trainers cannot answer that question. A shyness problem requires constant work to overcome, and with the number of commercials and films Melissa has done, we know the problem was solved. Melissa, with her expressive face, could emote better than Bette Davis. Like you, Susan wanted the public to see her dog perform, and what better way to do that than to give the dog theatrical training and chase elusive stardom?

Melissa is no longer with us, but Susan is still training dogs. Susan developed her own animal act in Walden, New York. Initially, she appeared as a clown but the makeup didn't help her allergies. Now she has two different acts, one featuring magic with the dogs and the other as a cowgirl. She knows the advantages of developing a couple of different acts. If you are doing children's parties, you get called back the next year with the other act. And the parents whose children are attending the party are often enthralled with the act, but they do not want the same act for the same group of children a few months later. The children don't care. They are enchanted with the animals even if the act is a repeat, but not the parents. The trainer uses the same animals, but with modified tricks and costuming it becomes two distinct acts. Susan had gotten dog-training jobs from her act, which is great. Where else can you get paid for advertising your business? Susan is looking for a replacement pig in her act. She thinks pigs are great. They are easier to train than dogs. Susan has even gotten pig-training jobs from her act.

## ★ BOB MARTWICK

Bob Martwick owned a kennel in the outskirts of Chicago. Living that close to a major metropolitan area, it was only natural that Bob would drift in to supplying animals for a lot of Chicago's film and TV industry. Martwick was looking for a cat when he strolled into the Hinsdale Animal Shelter and spotted an orange-striped cat. Trainers develop an eye for great dogs and cats. A quick look cues you. They have the right look. The élan, charisma, star quality. A second look and you can tell about their personality. Then you have to determine how they will behave around strange sights and sounds and how they relate to people. You develop the eye. How do you do it? I like to explain that any five-year-old can do it—with twenty years' experience. Actually not everyone has it, but Bob Martwick certainly has the eye. When he walked into that shelter he knew he had a cat that was different. He knew the cat had style. Never in his wildest dreams did Bob think that he was checking out the first feline superstar, Morris! The Leo Burnett advertising agency in Chicago was looking for a cat for a 9-Lives cat food commercial. They weren't looking for a "spokescat." They were looking for a cat in a commercial. Once they got film on Morris they knew that they had something very special. Bob Martwick kept busy with Morris. The kennel he had is now a shopping center. Such is progress in America today. Both he and Morris lived about twenty minutes, on a good day, from Chicago. Morris had to be available to pursue his career.

Morris was a real star. He had star quality. Everyone enjoyed working with him. "Morris is the most attentive co-star I've ever worked with," remarked Dyan Cannon.

## ★ TIM WELCH

It's time for Tim Welch to suit up. Before he starts getting into uniform, and it is a brightly colored uniform, he has to put on his proprietary makeup. Tim is a clown with Welch's Sheltie Circus. No, not "a" clown, "the" clown. The other performers are Shetland Sheepdogs . . . and a Cairn Terrier. If you were to ask Tim he would tell you that he is a dog trainer. I knew Tim when he was merely a dog lover. He had his Shelties and he wanted to get them into commercials. They lived in rural Pennsylvania and were not close enough to New York to become involved in the razzle-dazzle hustling that is so characteristic of the Big Apple. He would travel in. It didn't matter. He, like you, wanted the public to share in the joy his Shelties gave him. I gave him some general information and guidance—nowhere near as much as you are getting in this book. There just was not that much time. People like Tim are the reason for this book. Tim did it on his own. He designed and developed his act. Now he has forty-five minutes of circus performance tricks. He knows that he can adjust the act for those requiring shorter performances. His father built many of the props that he needed for his circus. He did commercials for a local department store. He started slowly, but his persistence paid off. In a recent month he did eleven shows. Not a record, but much better than a pretty good average in Thompson, Pennsylvania. Putting on shows prompted requests from local dog owners to train their dogs, so he started training dogs for other people.

\*    \*    \*

Where do you get ideas for your animal act? Take the time to see as many acts as you can. It may take a little travel time and effort. Have a vivid imagination. Go wild. Don't be limited by what you feel your animals can do. Figure out what you would like to see, then figure out how to do it. Remember that the tricks that impress most audiences are the ones with style and flair, and the truth of the matter is that these tricks are usually not the hardest to teach. The hardest tricks do not impress the general public; they do not realize the hard work that went into them.

A simple prop can add a lot to a trick. The manufacture of that prop may take more time than teaching your pet the trick for which it was manufactured. Also important is how you string the exercises together, and how you present them. Having a dog do a "dead dog" exercise can be spiced up by using the command "bang!" with the hand signal of your hand cocked like a gun. If you are in show business, the presentation is important.

Tim also competes in AKC obedience trials. He can't make any money doing that, but he enjoys the competition. Should anyone want to know if his dogs can do the job, those AKC obedience titles certainly qualify his animals. Tim is moving on up. Has he made his million yet? No, but he and his dogs are happy! That's the important thing.

## ★ PAUL GOLDIE

Paul Goldie is a very successful computer programmer by day. By night he turns into supertrainer. No, he doesn't shout a magic word to cause this transmogrification. He talks softly to one of his dogs and the dog is cued to play the role of Sandy in the musical *Annie*. You have to know a little bit about Paul to understand why he turns his back on easier, more lucrative pursuits to work with theatrical dogs. You know how well computer programmers are paid—much better than animal trainers. Paul has to be successful to live in exclusive Basking Ridge, New Jersey. He has a background in music and has played professionally. Paul is a producer in his own right. He was bitten by the showBiz bug a long time ago. He is also an animal lover. When a local theater company was staging a production of *Annie* he had a dog that would fill the bill. His music background let him know that training was important. He contacted Louise Auger of Auger's Canine College in New Jersey to give him some help in training his Sandy-type dog. Ahhhh, the smell of the greasepaint, the roar of the crowd! He was bitten again! Not by a flea but by that special showBiz bug that only bites animal lovers. Paul loved the challenge. He heard that I trained the original dog for the Broadway production and came to me for additional training. While working together he decided to get another Sandy dog. A backup dog. Paul filled a need. A dog, with backup, specially trained to perform *Annie*. It was far superior to the hit-or-miss method of hiring a local dog to do the exercises the script required.

Paul Goldie is a diligent, logical man. Excellent requirements for a computer programmer! Or a theatrical dog trainer. He obtained insurance, formed a corporation, hired an assistant, printed up business cards and took off. Now he juggles his vacation time from programming work to handling Sandy in *Annie*. At this writing Paul's stable consists of four dogs, three of which are trained to do *Annie*. Four or five times he has supplied dogs to more than one *Annie* at the same time. Duffy, one of his dogs, did two different productions on the same day. He has done over forty *Annie*s. Paul has directed *Annie* professionally three times. He loves the stage work more than the more lucrative TV or film work, but he isn't married to *Annie* and he has done other animal studio work. He has the luxury of picking and choosing his jobs and leans toward the stage work. If there are any "angels" reading this, Paul has a musical that he produced, which got very favorable reviews and which he is currently rewriting. Martin Charnin, the moving force behind the original *Annie*, may have some competition in the wings. If you are doing an *Annie*, there is no one better to get a Sandy from, not even me!

## ★ RALPH HELFER

Ralph Helfer was a kid from Chicago who loved animals. At age sixteen, while working in a pet shop, he had his first crack at "How to Get Your Pet Into Show Business." A production company needed two scorpions and Ralph supplied them. This job netted him fifty cents and whetted his appetite for bigger and better animal assignments—and bigger animals. Chicago is not the best place to keep a menagerie, but Ralph became one of the world's most successful wild-animal trainers, even eclipsing the synonym for wild-animal trainer, Frank Buck. Today Ralph regularly commutes between Los Angeles and Africa after a distinguished career that includes eighteen Patsies (the animal equivalent of Academy Award); over 5,000 movies, TV shows and commercials as well as other projects involving animals; and developing and establishing Marineworld/Africa, USA. His animals have appeared in such classic films as *The Greatest Show on Earth* and *The Ten Commandments.* On television "Gentle Ben," "Daktari" and "Charley's Angels" have been graced with the Helfer hand. Ralph has as his logo/slogan "Affection Training," which he feels is his most important contribution to the industry.

Like many other animal trainers, he revels in the stunt work that he has done. Working with animals presents many opportunities to do stunt work. Stunt work is all part of that showBiz glamour, and I enjoy listening to stunt players talk about the various jobs they have done. I even enjoy talking about the stunt work I have done. It is even more glamorous than being a . . . mere actor. A dangerous adventure. Working with various wild animals, Ralph Helfer had many occasions to put his life on the line. The full-time stunt man who feels that he can also handle being attacked by animals may be making a mistake. Most stunt players specialize in various "gags," but then there are the stunt men who, like actors, feel they can do everything. No one is an expert in it all. Ralph Helfer is an expert in being attacked by wild animals.

# ★ JOE PHILLIPS

Cowboy Joe Phillips has more than an animal act. It is a western act, a western show. Joe sings, strums a guitar, ropes, juggles guns and takes three cuts with a bull whip on a cigarette held in someone's mouth. This kind of variety makes an act interesting. Goldie, the dancing horse, knows more dance steps than Fred Astaire. Bullet the Wonder Dog and Peaches the Computer Dog round out Joe's act. The ten-gallon hat, the cowboy boots and the two six-shooters strapped to his sides would tell you that Joe comes from "Deep in the Heart of Texas." Joe's home town has a Native American name, but the truth of the matter is that his "ranch" is out on Long Island, in Lake Ronkonkoma, New York. This is in keeping with showBiz tradition. "Bronco Billie" Anderson, the silent screen's first cowboy hero, was also a New Yorker. Joe was fifteen when he bought his first horse. His love of horses drew him to the dude ranches where he worked and started developing his horse-training skills. He competed in rodeos. (Why do these animal trainers always like to take life-threatening risks?) Joe developed and performed his act at rodeos, but those in charge quickly put a stop to his calf-roping competition. They were afraid he would get so badly banged up that he wouldn't be able to do his show. He has been doing his act far longer than he would like to admit. It is never the same act. He is continually revising it so it flows. How has Joe done over the years with his animal act? Well, don't try to call him in the mornings. He is out on the golf course seven days a week.

# How to Be a Pro

"All the world's a
stage,
And all the men
and women
merely players."

**Shakespeare**

There is a cast of players that you will be dealing with in showBiz. While the information that follows deals primarily with film and TV, it is applicable to all phases of the business. Knowing who you are dealing with can be confusing, but it is *extremely* important. Jobs and responsibilities overlap, which adds to the confusion.

## ★ THE PRODUCER

The producer is the money man in all cases except the majority of cases. A contradiction? Yes, but true. You can be a producer if you have a film, play, animal act or TV show and have the money to put it together. The producer is responsible for everything from inception of the idea to its completion, and in the case of a film, the release, promotion and residual sales. In today's megabuck film industry, the producer would approach a studio with a package he has put together and the studio would come up with the money. Without a track record, the producer will probably

35

see no money and the project will go down the tubes. A good package would consist of a great script written by a successful writer, a name director, a top-flight star and, in film, a top-of-the-line director of photography. The commitments have to be firm in a business where nothing is set in stone. You will never get all these great people together at one time. They have too many irons in the fire. The big film is always changing.

In TV the producer does not usually have a financial responsibility but must handle administration, costs and overseeing the end quality of the program. In TV commercials technically the client is the producer, but many of these responsibilities trickle down to the production company. The production company works for the ad agency, who works for the client.

There are a number of different kinds of producers, such as the executive producer, who can be a titular head; the line producer, who is responsible for the day-to-day shooting, and the ordinary, everyday producer. Growing budgets have taken a lot of the authority out of the hands of producers compared to the earlier years in the business. Current trends in the film business put young and inexperienced directors under the guidance and control of a knowledgeable producer. The time of the *auteur* has passed because of the complexities and costs of the business; the producer can be the most creative person on a project.

## ★ THE DIRECTOR

The director is the one who directs the play, film, TV pilot, animal act or other project. You work directly with the director but may not get a chance to talk to him until the day of the shoot, both for film and TV commercials.

This is one of the problems in the business: Those in specialized areas, like animal handlers/trainers, do not communicate with the director until the eleventh hour. This lack of communication is a handicap. The animal handler should be on board during preproduction and rehearsal so that shots can be discussed and set up. There should be a discussion of the animal's capabilities and limitations. On the day of shooting, it is too late to attempt some specialized training with your creative canine.

Once I was working on an "After School Special" TV film in Colorado. We had traveled there for the snow. We were shooting above the timberline. That's where the air is so thin that trees cannot grow. The aptly named "Snowbound" was on an unbelievable shooting schedule, with eighteen-hour days in freezing weather that sapped everyone's energy. Robert M. Young, a brilliant director, was working at an unreal pace and didn't have time to think. I tried to speak with him on a number of occasions, but his time was so taken up he couldn't talk to me. Rather than becoming frustrated, I kept saying to myself, "Well, he's going to have to talk to me sooner or later." When it was time to film the dog work, we got to talk and it came off without a hitch. That was very late in the game to discuss just exactly what the dogs were to do. The competent handler/trainer will anticipate, and prepare for, all the variables. Initial communications are often handled by a PA, or production assistant, the lowest of the low. They are even ranked below you. PAs can't answer your questions, but you are supposed to answer their questions, and they are asking the wrong ones. PAs are generally overworked, underpaid people eager to get into film. In other cases they are less dedicated kids who are friends of a friend. This friend-of-a-friend syndrome is more common in Hollywood, the company town, than in New York.

# ★ THE ART DIRECTOR

You might have contact with the art director, the person responsible for the appearance and texture of the world in which the project appears. Animals certainly have a great deal to do with the film's overall appearance. The art director will be as difficult to get hold of as the director.

# ★ THE CLIENT

The client is one step below God, unless you are the advertising agency, which considers the client as one step *above* God. The client is the firm paying for the whole *megillah* and is peculiar to TV commercials or other advertising or promotional projects developed by the advertising agency. The client is the one with the product or service that is being promoted.

# ★ THE ADVERTISING AGENCY

The advertising agency is employed by the client. The ad agency comes up with the overall ad campaign for the client. When you think about firms that spend over $400 million a year, such as McDonald's, AT&T and Sears, you know they are dealing with a customer they do not want to lose. The ad agency hires the production company that makes the commercial.

# ★ THE PRODUCTION COMPANY

The production company is exactly that. It produces the commercial. They are given the money by the ad agency, who oversees the spending of money, as well as everything else. On smaller accounts in smaller cities the ad agency may act as a production company. All of these roles can overlap, depending on the size of the account.

# ★ CASTING DIRECTORS, ETC.

The *casting director* usually does not handle hiring the animals, but in some cases does. Casting directors are not always used on commercials. The job is often handled by the ad agency and/or the director and/or the production company. On feature films a casting director is used, and in the last few years the top ones have become prominent and powerful. Animals are handled by props and wardrobe in the AICP Production Cost Summary. However, animals can be ordered by just about anyone.

To avoid any confusion, let's first distinguish between a casting director and an *agent*. A casting director works for the film company, generally as a subcontractor, on a percentage of payroll basis or for an agreed-upon flat rate. Casting directors get the best talent at the best prices. An agent, on the other hand, works for the actor and tries to get said actor an interview with the casting director. It is not the agent's job to get the actor the job. That is the actor's job. Getting the actor the best deal possible is the agent's job. An agent is the person who complains about an actor getting the other 90 percent of the agent's money. They are the subject of jokes, as in "What is the difference between a dead agent and a dead skunk on a road? There are skid marks in front of the skunk." As to the number of agents required to screw in a light bulb? "I'll get back to you!" and she or he never does. Now that we know what casting directors and agents are, let's discuss *managers*. Managers handle (or mishandle) an actor's career. They generally take 25 percent. A top-flight actor with more work than he can handle needs a manager to keep him on the right track career wise and the right work money wise. The manager tries to get the actor in to see the right people. A *business manager* will take care of all bills, etc., and put the actor on an allowance. Actors who don't watch their manager can, and do, get into financial binds. In the eyes of an actor, a current manager is the best in the world, while an ex-manager is a thief.

# ★ THE ANIMAL AGENCY

The animal agency is in truth a packager, an entity that puts together all the animal work. Human actors' agents are limited to a 10 percent commission, according to union regulations and some state laws. Animal agencies give the production company a price and then proceed to line up the animals and handlers needed to do the job. They have the necessary licenses and insurance coverage for the job. They are responsible for the coordination of transportation, grooming, rehearsal, prepping the animals, etc. (The animal agency may turn all of this over to an individual animal owner they hire as a subcontractor.) In construction they would be referred to as a "general contractor." They are on the bottom of the showBiz hierarchy, or perhaps the top of the lowerarchy. You are even lower because you are under the animal agent.

*Caution!* There are animal agencies and animal agencies. You want to work for an agency that is licensed by the United States Department of Agriculture so that you are under their protection. Firms exist that do not really own, train, store, keep and/or maintain animals but do book animals. They probably are not licensed.

# ★ RULES ON THE SET

You are going on the set for the very first time. The night before you can't sleep because of the anticipated excitement. You have no trouble getting up even without a decent night's sleep. You are about as relaxed as a football locker room at halftime. You hastily dress. You know you have to be there on time. You have everything ready and you start loading the car. Don't forget your favorite animal. The animal is your *raison d'être.* As you approach your destination, your tension rises a few more notches. Soon you will be entering the holiest of holies. That cathedral of commerce that creates the TV commercial or feature film. It may be a print job creating a slick, glowing ad or maybe even a stage play. It has dark corners contrasting with the brightly lit sets. As soon as you get there, report to the animal agency you are working for or to the assistant director. It is your job to let the production company know that you, especially if you are representing an animal agency, are there. Checking in early is so important that if practical leave the animal locked in the car when you check in. Remember to leave the motor on with heat or air conditioning working, depending on the weather. Your pet must be secured so that it cannot kick the car in gear. *Take a spare key!* There is nothing wrong with being logged in early, but there is much wrong with being late.

I was supplying a dog in Connecticut for a film directed by the great Elia Kazan. It was a long drive from New York City, with an early departure time. Every day we got there and sat around waiting to go to work. Driving there very early one morning, we were a little ahead of schedule, and I was famished. I knew we would be sitting around waiting for everything to be set up when we got there, so I decided to stop and eat, and I pulled into a diner. My assistant, Flo Boese, said, "We'll be late." We were—

five minutes late! Kazan greeted me with, "You're late!" I haven't been late since.

Ask where you can set up with your pet. Your next move after your animal is settled is to get "coffee and." That table with food is for you as well as others on the job, unless there is a sign up advising you otherwise. Dig in!

Everyone else seems so calm. They have done this hundreds, even thousands, of times, and it is old hat. There is another reason that they don't have their nerves strung out like you. They keep busy! You can avoid performance anxiety if you keep busy. Watch some of the actors do stretching, loosening-up and relaxation exercises. No one stares at them. Everyone on the set has seen actors doing these strange gyrations. Nothing you do will be considered too strange. Watch the teamsters. They can have a bagel in one hand, a cup of coffee in the other hand, and hold a tabloid with their other hands. That's relaxation developed to a science. Bring something to read even if you feel nervous. Bring this book along for quick reference. Grooming your animal and preparing it for the job is another activity that can and should keep you busy. Grooming will relax you and your animal. Prepping your pet should be uppermost in your mind. Take a walk around the set with your future star. Do some relaxation exercises for your cat. Scratch its tummy.

There are a number of rules on the set. Let's start with the "don'ts."

**1.** Don't make noise. Keep quiet!

**2.** Don't get in the way.

**3.** Don't ask questions.

**4.** Don't *answer* questions.

**5.** Don't ask for autographs.

**6.** Don't sit on a set.

**7.** Don't even go near a "hot" set.

**8.** Don't lean on anything.

**9.** Don't wear socks with holes in them.

**10.** Don't leave the set unless you tell the head wrangler or assistant director.

**11.** Don't discuss costs or prices with anyone on the set.

**12.** Don't hand out your business card unless this is *your* job.

**13.** Don't carry a camera.

**14.** Don't ask for copies of photographs taken.

**15.** Don't be a pest.

**16.** Don't wear makeup, after-shave or perfume, particularly when working with exotics.

**17.** Don't wear jewelry.

**18.** Don't use drugs, booze or cigarettes when working with animals.

After all those don'ts, you are entitled to some "do's":

**1.** Do wear comfortable and informal clean clothes.

**2.** Do pay attention to what is going on.

**3.** Do bring an assistant.

**4.** Do anticipate what is happening.

**5.** Do make and take an equipment kit.

**6.** Do position yourself so the animal is facing properly.

**7.** Do take the animal in and out the same way.

**8.** Do rehearse every chance you get.

**9.** Do use the Captain Haggerty Key Light Cuing System if applicable (see Appendix 2).

**10.** Do behave at least as well as your pet.

Now as to the whys and wherefores of these rules. First the don'ts.

**1.** Don't make noise. Keep quiet! Even if it is for a still shot in which there is no sound take. Other people on the set are attempting to concentrate and communicate. They should not have to do that over your voice. The business is frantic enough, and on the set everyone tries to keep things as calm as possible. Useless prattle does not contribute to the success of the project.

**2.** Don't get in the way. Watch out for that camera lens. A smidgen of your shoulder within the camera frame means a ruined shot. A shadow from your head means a ruined shot. Get out of the way of technicians moving equipment. Do not trip over the cable. Keep alert and watch where you are stepping. Do not break an actor's line of sight. Do not stand in view of the actor. If he blows his lines he will blame you for standing there. Never, never distract anyone who is working.

3. Don't ask questions. People are busy and they do not want to educate you in their complex business. Of course you can talk to people, but only if they approach you first. They will want to talk to you about animals, and if you can steer the conversation around to a showBiz subject that you are interested in, fine. Let them initiate and lead the conversation. The Good Lord gave you two ears and one mouth. There is a message there.

4. Don't *answer* questions. It sounds like a strange rule, but there are good reasons for it. All questions should be referred to the animal agency/head wrangler/ handler/trainer unless you are on the job by yourself. Even an innocuous question as to the animal's age can cause a problem if someone else has given a different figure. Age and name are the two most frequently asked questions. Those working with your pet should know these answers. Geriatric dogs are not wanted on the set. ShowBiz is ruled by the young. A nine-year-old dog that is the picture of health will get the negative reaction of "I didn't order an aged and decrepit dog." And if it is for a dog food commercial that brags about how long this dog has been eating the product, you'll still get in trouble. The dog is too young. Amazing but true! This is potentially a dangerous question.

5. Don't ask for autographs. This is sure suicide on the set. The best way to make everyone your enemy is to ask the star for his or her autograph. Some stars (particularly soap stars) are more than happy to accommo-

date you—but only after *they* have initiated a conversation about animals and their pet python Peter. At that point tell them how much you "have enjoyed their work." That's the accepted terminology. If you can think of a specific role they played that impressed you, that is even better. Recalling the little pieces of business they developed in an obscure file will endear you to them. Now you are buddies. Now spring your trap. "I don't normally do this and I hate to bother you, but my niece also thinks you're terrific and I know she would love your autograph, if it isn't too much trouble. Oh, ahhh, umm, yes, she has the same name as mine. She was named after me."

6. Don't sit on a set. If when sitting down in a chair you move it one millimeter, you will louse up the lighting on the actor's face. Sets are not for sitting unless you are an on-camera actor who is working in the scene.

7. Don't even go near a "hot" set. Don't even look at one. A "Hot Set" sign will be on this set, but assume that all sets are hot sets. A hot set is one in which everything is set perfectly and on which the shooting is imminent. The set may have already been filmed, and you, by moving a book, upset continuity.

8. Don't lean on anything. That solid stone wall holding back tons of earth will fall over on you if you lean on it. It's not stone, it's papier-mâché.

9. Don't wear socks with holes in them. When photographing on "no seam" (long rolls of colored paper), you have to take off your shoes so the paper is not covered with tracks. Remember when your mother told you to wear clean underwear when you go outside, in case you get hit by a truck. Don't embarrass

your mother, yourself or me. Should you get caught with a hole in your sock, don't tell anybody you read this book. The chances of being required to take your shoes off is greater than getting hit by a truck.

10. Don't leave the set unless you tell the head wrangler or assistant director. Don't go to the bathroom, don't make a phone call, don't go to the caterer's table without clearing it first. If you were hired by an animal agency and they are on the set, you can clear it with them. Should you be needed, they can fill in before you get back. Do not dilly-dally. The assistant director is the correct person to ask, but it will take him a little time to get the answer. As long as you have someone there to jump in with your animal, you are covered. Come *right* back!

11. Don't discuss costs or prices with anyone on the set. People don't usually ask, but occasionally you will find a nosy person. If you are working for someone else you will not know the answer anyway. You know what you are getting paid, but you do not know what is being charged. It is extremely bad form to mention what you and your pet are paid. It doesn't matter what the animal agency is getting paid. That is their business and not yours. If you want to become an agent and worry about insurance, rent, answering services, advertising, people that don't show up and the myriad of problems in the business, then read on. We will tell you how to do that, too. In the meantime do not worry about the end price. This is the easiest question to turn aside. Just say, "I don't know. I didn't quote the job." If you want to put a topper on that, try "I'm sure you got a good deal with all the preproduction work we put in on this job."

The Andy Warhol film *Bad* had a scene in which a

baby was thrown out of a window and lands "splat" on the sidewalk. They wanted a dog to go up to the doll that was supposed to be the dead baby and sniff at the entrails. It was an easy job. I felt the scene was too gross. I refused to do it. I wasn't told about it beforehand and had no obligation to do the job. They managed to get an actress who was working on the film to do the job with her dog. I made the social gaffe of asking how much she was getting paid for the dog. I want everyone to be well paid. She refused to tell me. When she found out who I was, she wanted to ask me how to do the job and how much money she should get. The shoe was now on the other foot. There is an old show Business maxim: "Be nice to the people you meet on the way up, because you will meet them on the way down."

12. Don't hand out your business card unless this is *your* job. I know you breed Basenjis and the animal agency does not. There is no competition there. You are expecting a litter next month and one of the grips just doesn't know where to find the dog of his dreams: An African breed that doesn't bark and comes into heat once a year. Clear giving your card out with the animal agency or tell the grip he should contact the animal agency directly. You are working for the animal agency, and it is their customer. If you tell the agency how you handled it, they will feel happier working with you. The agency will refer the grip back to you for the pup.

13. Don't carry a camera. I know you are not going to follow this caveat. If you have to carry a camera, make sure it is one of the inexpensive automatic cameras in the $100 price range. If you show up with professional

equipment you are going to upset a lot of people, particularly if it is a union job. Only union photographers are supposed to be on the job. I know you didn't listen, so now I will tell you how to disobey this rule. Do not use a flash. It is too obvious but more important the flash can screw up some of the cameras and equipment. There is no need for lighting on a set that is perfectly lit by pros. The lighting is flawless. Go back and reread item 5. If the star loves your dog, cat, llama or ostrich, offer to take a picture of him with it. Explain that you will send a copy to him and do it. You'll have the negative and the picture you want. There are four elements to any picture that you can take on the set. The animal, the star, the equipment and you. Getting all four elements in the picture is impossible. Three out of four ain't bad, and it tells a story. If you can't get two out of four, you do not need to take the picture.

14. Don't ask for copies of photographs taken. The still photographer is working for the film company or production company. Some of the photographs will be used for lobby cards, publicity stills and other promotional purposes. They are easier to get after the film is released, but you will have to make a lot of phone calls to find the right person to help you. Leaving a message does not mean that your call will be returned. Once you have found the right person, you are in Fat City. You may have a chance to see *all* the stills and have your wants made for you. Always offer to pay for them. You may not have to but the offer should be an honest one, and some greedy person dealing with the pictures may look at it as a way to make a couple of bucks. If that person helps you, so much the better. If it is a high-fashion still photographer taking the pic-

tures, approach the photographer in the same way. He may have some pictures that were not used that he will give you. If given a firm "no!" fold your tent and slink away. Do not become a pest.

15. Don't be a pest. Don't be a pest! Don't be a pest!!! Read all of the above. Don't get in anybody's way. When they are ready to shoot, your conversation ends, even in midsentence. Be unobtrusive. Be invisible. Don't be a pest!

16. Don't wear makeup, after-shave or perfume, particularly when working with exotics. Their odor can distract the animals. Bright red lipstick can be a further visual distraction. Women undergoing their menstrual period can be a further distraction, and in some cases, with some animals, it can be dangerous.

17. Don't wear jewelry. Not only can rings, earrings, eyeglasses, etc., be distracting to the animal, but also those animals with "hands" may grab at them. In the case of pierced earrings, it can be disastrous. There is the further danger of having the jewelry catch on something. When possible, eyeglasses and sunglasses should also be avoided. Sunglasses obscure the animal's ability to see your eyes.

18. Don't use drugs, booze or cigarettes when working with animals. The first two items should be obvious. Not only do alcohol and drugs impair your judgment and reflexes, but often they will upset the animal. Cigarette smoke can momentarily obscure the animal's and the handler's vision. An even more important reason is the danger of a hot ash hitting the animal.

Now to those "do's."

1. Do wear comfortable and informal clean clothes. I don't care how high tone the production company is, you do not wear a tux or evening clothes. You want to blend in. Jeans and a work shirt are fine. Look neat, not slovenly. Neatness counts. It looks professional, and that is what you want to be. If you look like a pro, they'll treat you like a pro. A lot of production people make a good dollar and certainly will be wearing designer jeans and upscale working clothes. Designer jeans are not a requirement. Comfortable shoes are a must. Rubber soles with a low heel are a good bet.

2. Do pay attention to what is going on. You want to learn. You'll hear the jargon, and that will make you even more of a pro. You'll get into the rhythm of the set and be able to do a better job.

3. Do bring an assistant. Not a friend from the neighborhood but someone who can genuinely help you when you need it. While it is not impossible for one person to do a job, it always runs smoother with two people. Two animals require three people, and if you follow the rule of one person per animal plus one you will be covered successfully. If you bring someone along who just wants to see what is happening, the production people will know you brought a tourist and will be unhappy. Give that tourist a job to do, make sure he or she does it and you will be home free. Make sure your assistant knows all the do's and don'ts.

   I did a Milk Bone commercial in midtown Manhattan that required eighty-seven puppies. It didn't require eighty-eight people but it did require a lot of people to man the mops and brooms. Remember, these were puppies. We did a great job of scheduling and brought more dogs than requested. Extra people cost us a little more money to do the job, but we wanted to do the job right. Everything ran smoothly. We were ahead of schedule. We continued to shoot after we had more than enough footage. I asked the director what the problem was. He said the client was pissed off. "Why?" I queried. "We gave them everything they wanted without a hitch. It went like clockwork." His answer was, "Yeah, but they could have gotten by if they rented the studio for just half a day." We did the job too well and too fast. They are never satisfied!

4. Do anticipate what is happening. Know in advance when they are going to call you and be ready. Send your assistant to get that special treat or that other piece of equipment.

5. Do make and take an equipment kit. Get a small bag and figure out what you are going to need for the job you are doing. Just keep adding to that bag and increasing the bag's size. If you needed it once, you will need it again. If you have a dog, a cat and a pelican, make a separate one for each animal. They have separate needs and require individual bags.

6. Do position yourself so the animal is facing properly. Your partner only has eyes for you. Position yourself and move yourself so that he is continually facing in the right direction. What does the script call for your animal to do? Which direction should the animal be facing and what should be the expression on his face? As mentioned in the last chapter, Susan Zaretsky, a very fine animal trainer/handler, had a random-bred dog named Melissa that worked a lot. Melissa, like many dogs, used to get into the litter box and eat the cat feces, for which she was continually scolded. Anytime Melissa was doing a film and needed a contrite expression on her face, Susan had a command. "Who

ate the cat sh——?" she would scold. Expression and
direction are very important. Nothing annoys me more
than the animal facing off-camera, in the wrong direction, looking at its trainer. Watch the work of veteran
trainer Frank Inn in the *Benji* films to see perfect performance with Benji never facing his handler.

7. Do take the animal in and out the same way. If an
animal is to run out a door stage left, bring it in and out
the same way. Do not show it any other way to make
the trip. If your dog or cat realizes that there is another
way to make the trip, he or she may take the wrong
route.

8. Do rehearse every chance you get. Try to find out in
advance which set you will be working on. Get permission to work your animal on that set and introduce
Bernie, your bashful bat, to the set. Find out exactly
what Bernie has to do and practice him on the set. Be
aware that the blocking can very well be changed when
it comes time to shoot.

9. Do use the Captain Haggerty Key Light Cuing System
if applicable (see Appendix 2).

10. Do behave at least as well as your pet. More is expected from you than your animal. I know your animal
is wonderful, but don't show it off. You are there to do
a job. Showing off is not only a distraction to those
working but may present some safety problems.

# ★ THE PRO'S ALMANAC

I can't tell you "how to succeed in show Business without really trying." There is no such animal. Being professional will make you successful. If you look like a pro, you will be a pro.

1. Stay at the end of the film and watch the credits.

2. Watch the pros. See how they handle and train animals. The best place to see this, although it is not directly connected with show Business handling, is at dog shows. Watch the Junior Showmanship Competition. Watch the professional handlers. Watch obedience.

3. Read everything. Even if you become so great that you only get one idea out of an entire book, that idea will be a gem. Read not only about animals, but also about show Business.

4. Be objective. Watching someone else work should be viewed objectively, not negatively.

5. Be positive. No one wants to work with or around negative people.

6. The amateurs do not observe their competition. The pros do.

7. Self-criticism, rather than criticism of others, is the road to improving your skills. Observe others, but do not criticize.

8. Take film, TV and stage courses. Take animal courses. Knowledge is power.

**9.** Read the trades. Show business and animal.

**10.** Immerse yourself in the business.

**11.** Be a fanatic on getting the shot. It is the most important thing in the world at that place and time.

**12.** Correction: The animal's safety and care come first. After that comes the shot.

**13.** Strive to be the best handler possible. On reaching that goal you can become more creative by approaching your contribution from a story-telling point of view.

**14.** Have a broad vision. Do not be myopic. Know and understand what everyone is doing and why.

**15.** Don't be a stage mother.

**16.** You have the toughest job in the business. The care, comfort and safety of the animals in your care is your constant task, twenty-four hours a day.

**17.** Look at the ads in magazines. Analyze how they are done. How can they be improved?

**18.** Analyze how everything is done. Rent films for your VCR and use the slow-motion and freeze-frame features to analyze how the animal shots were done.

**19.** In viewing animal work, where was the animal facing and why?

**20.** Look for the flaws in every TV show, commercial, photograph, etc. How could it be done better?

21. Learn about film editing and how it will affect your animal work. Study films, particularly action films, where stunt players are substituted for main actors.

22. After every job evaluate what you did right and wrong. Then move on to your next project.

23. A pro does not drop the leash or cat chain.

24. A pro doesn't use drugs, booze or cigarettes when working animals.

25. A pro does not show off.

26. Distance control and work is important. You should always work on extending the distance.

27. It is *your* responsibility to determine when an animal is overworked or tired. This is important for the animal's safety and well-being. In the case of a dangerous animal it is important for the safety and well-being of cast and crew. Do not be afraid to stop the action when necessary. You are the expert!

28. Always carry and hand out business cards. If you are doing the job for someone else, do *not* give out your personal card. You are working under somebody's banner and those are the cards to hand out. If someone wants to get in touch with you, they will do it through your boss. Explain that to both parties and they will respect you for it.

29. Always carry a theatrical kit for each animal. Add to the kit continually. If you used it before, you will need it again. If working for yourself emblazon your name on the case.

**30.** A pro is always on time. Arrive a half hour before your scheduled reporting time. If travel time is more than one hour and forty-five minutes, arrive an hour earlier. If travel time is more than three hours, arrive the previous day.

**31.** A pro, when working on a stage play, continually improves her or his animal's performance. The true pro tries to add training and business to the animal's part, in effect padding the part.

**32.** A pro always tries to do better.

# The Training Course

"This is the start
of your educa-
tion."

Al Pacino as Lt.
Col. Frank Slade
in *Scent of a
Woman*

You started off right! You bought this book. Now what should your pet be able to do? Everything! I can't count the number of times I have gone on a set with the understanding that "the dog just has to stand there." The director then says, "Have the dog leap into the burning building, carry the baby out to safety, guard the baby until the firemen give it artificial respiration, then chase the truck that the pyromaniac is escaping in, leap into the back, climb up on the roof and crawl to the cab, where the dog will subdue and disarm the criminal while bringing the truck to a safe halt." If you say that you were told the dog was just supposed to stand there, you get asked, "Isn't this a trained dog? Well, maybe we can forget about the dog bringing the truck to a safe halt. I'll see if I can get a stunt man to do that!" But this isn't just about dogs.

Conditioning, training, socializing, teaching, desensitizing. No matter what you call it, your wonderful wombat must be prepared. Your precious pet should perform anywhere. The way to do that is to train it everywhere. Shopping centers, Times Square, in the middle of World War III. Busy streets, busy traffic and even on the location where the tape or film is to be shot. The actual location is perking with preoccupied people moving in and out, delivering and picking up, buying and selling, fixing and repairing, plus everything else that is done on an actual location. They will not and cannot shut the location down for your practice prior to performance. Stopping by on a busy day, before shooting begins, will acclimate and desensitize your pet to the location. If the people that are renting the location know that you are with the production company, they may feel that they are entitled to more money, so be cautious. "More money" is the dirtiest word in the book, according to production companies. Don't even mention it in polite company! The preparation for a dog is quite a bit different from that of a Madeira cockroach. Let's see what training some animals should have.

## ★ DOGS

This book starts with the basic assumption that if you have a dog, he is obedience trained. He already knows General Obedience commands as a minimum training requirement. Remember, we expect more from dogs than from any other animal. Dogs are the most highly domesticated animal after humans ... or some humans! If you are an obedience buff or even an obedience pro, we are home free. If your dog doesn't have that level of training, don't worry. Be happy! I'll outline and show you how to get your dog this training and expand on that training with the goal of working in showBiz.

Your dog is smart, civilized, responsive. He loves to perform parlor tricks. You're into challenging him. You like experimenting. You work well together. You enjoy amusing your friends. Applause from a receptive audience spurs both of you to new heights. You're born performers. In other words, you're hams!

How do you get training? There are five basic ways in which you can accomplish training:

1. Read a book. Unfortunately, less than 5 percent of the people can *obedience* train a dog from a book. Dog obedience training books are excellent supplemental material and can focus your thinking before, during and after training your dog. Dog tricks *can* be taught from a book once your dog has been obedience trained and is performing for you. You might want to consult *Dog Tricks,* a book I co-authored with Carol Lea Benjamin.

2. Videotapes are better than books, providing you view each exercise individually, stop the tape and work your dog on that exercise prior to going on to the next exercise. Obedience training has to be structured. Trick training does not have to be as structured as obedience training, unless you are building on the previous exercise. As you progress and *you* learn how to teach each exercise, expand to teaching a couple of tricks at a time. Again, as you progress and *you* have learned to teach the trick, it is time to work on a couple of exercises at once. Videos, the newest of training methods are growing in popularity and they, along with books, provide excellent supplemental information. I recommend, without reservation, the dog trick videos I have done. (Write to P.O. Box 3462, Beverly Hills, CA 90212 for information.)

3. Group lessons, for teaching obedience, are available everywhere. There are all-breed dog clubs, obedience clubs, humane societies and private individuals that give these courses. While proponents of group classes stress the importance of being trained with your dog and working around other dogs as a distraction, only

60 percent of the people taking the group classes *successfully* complete the course. Exposure to other dogs is a plus, providing your dog is not so distracted that nothing can be accomplished. There are some areas in the country where people are teaching group classes in trick work and theatrical or studio work.

4. Private lessons are the most effective method of training you and your dog. You receive personalized one-on-one training, which is so very important if you are to handle your dog in a theatrical situation. A reminder: They have to train you to train your dog. If the choice is between private lessons in the home and going to the trainer, choose the latter. The end results are much better. Your attitude is different when you are sitting on your favorite living room chair with a drink in your hand completely relaxed. You are not ready to work with your dog. However, after driving twenty minutes and arriving on the trainer's doorstep with your dog in the heel position, you are in gear and mentally ready to train!

5. Board and training is a much-maligned way to have your dog trained. Results are excellent as long as you are shown how to handle your dog after the training is completed. For a busy person who does not have time to work his or her dog, this is the preferred way. But if you do not have time to train your dog, when are you going to find time to handle the dog when your big show Business break occurs? Another variation of the board and training is a day care program, where you drop Roscoe off for training in the morning and pick him up at night.

   All things considered, number four is the best approach to take. Where do we go after the obedience course? To more advanced training. Where do you get this more advanced training? It now becomes difficult to get that one-on-one instruction needed for theatrical training. Some trainers look disparagingly at dog tricks. Often it is fear of the unknown that dissuades people from teaching trick work. This becomes a stumbling block for *you*. You want a trainer who is not only willing to teach you tricks but also has experience. A compromise would be to work with a competition-driven trainer who will teach you open and utility work, which is a viable alternative to the trick work.

What level of training should the theatrical dog attain? Everyone claims that his or her dog is well trained. Do you want to go on a set or go for a print job and have your dog embarrass you? Even with well-trained dogs, we sometimes run into problems. I never have any problem with untrained dogs. I just don't take them with me. Minimum training is basic obedience, but what is basic obedience? The exercises that are necessary for a dog to get a Companion Dog (C.D.) degree from the American Kennel Club or a United-Companion Dog (U-C.D.) from the United Kennel Club. The requirements, while basically similar for each organization, do have some differences. These terms are understood by dog trainers, and if you are seeking professional help they will know what they mean. Does your dog need a training degree to go into show business? It wouldn't hurt. The training degrees are not necessary. The level of training is.

In addition to obedience we teach the dog to bark on cue, tug at an object, head up, head down, grab a pants' leg, paws up, say your prayers, pad work, sit high and beg, balance a piece of food on the nose and catch it on command. Hand signals are stressed throughout. The dog must be able to retrieve any object on demand. Pad work is training a dog to grab and hold on to a 5 x 5-inch burlap pad. While similar to a retrieving exercise, the motivation is different, thus producing a different appearance and theatrical effect.

# ★ A TRICK COURSE OUTLINE

**TRICK COURSE I**   Paws Up, Say Your Prayers, Shake Hands, Balance and Catch, Sit High (Beg), Speak, Play Dead and Roll Over.

**TRICK COURSE II**   Introduction to Retrieving, Zig Zag (Shine My Shoes), Count and Do Math, Crawl, Introduction to Limp, Food Refusal, Tug It, Introduction to Scent Discrimination (Smell It, Find It), Stick Jumping and Plotz (which is the down position with the dog's head on ground between legs).

**TRICK COURSE III**   Further Work on Retrieving, The Seek Back (Finding Lost Articles), Limp, Walk on Hindquarters (Dance, Cha-Cha-Cha, Waltz, etc.), Jump Through a Hoop, Salute, Jump Over Arms and Jump Over Back of Owner.

**THEATRICAL TRAINING**   The above trick courses are excellent. They make for a lot of fun and are a starting point for theatrical/studio work. Other tricks, which are extremely desirable for the theatrical dog and which I teach to dogs that have graduated from the above courses are: Grab and Pull on a Trouser Leg, Scratch (itself), Sneeze, Pad Work, Heel on the Right Side, Dig, Jump Up on Actor, Paw and Nudge Actor and Back Up.

I've pioneered these unique courses, but it isn't necessary for a dog to be under my tutelage to get into show Business, and here's why:

1. Most jobs can be handled with a general obedience course.

2. Any advanced training will put your dog a few notches above the competition.

3. There are many fine trainers out there who will teach "tricks."

4. Once you have handled a dog through the basic obedience, you can go on to additional training yourself, using books and videos to guide you. Stick with a professional trainer as long as practical.

5. As you do additional training with your dog, you become a better handler. Remember that handling is more important than training for theatrical dogs.

Follow a progression from General Obedience to Open and Utility work or Trick Dog I, II and III and Theatrical Training as outlined above. You will have a well-trained dog that can handle just about any situation. Lacking that, you can have the smartest dog in your neighborhood and delight all the kids.

Is this the way I train one of my own theatrical dogs? No, I keep the dog with me twenty-four hours a day. We hang out together, and I am continually giving the dog a two- or three-minute training session. It is completely unstructured and works for me. It will not work for you until you get a lot more training time under your leash. Stick with a structured program.

# ★ CATS

Check out some of those cat training books. They contain good information, although most authors are telling you what they did with one great cat that the good Lord or Lady Luck gave them. The cat should sit, stay, come, exit at two and preferably three different speeds, jump up on different objects, beg or sit up on their hindquarters and paw an object.

A cat can be trained to do these things, but it takes more time than it does for a dog. The fact that people feel that cats cannot be trained is a plus for you. They can be trained! Learn what motivates cats so that you can not only train them but also handle them on the set.

Cats are predators. Use that instinct to get a performance. All sorts of devices entrance cats and kittens. They should be standard items carried in your cat's case or your kitten's kit. The simplest device is a piece of string with a small piece of paper tied to the end. Drag that across the floor and you certainly will get the cat's attention.

The rat and mouse are the cat's quarry. Rats and mice are readily available and can be easily transported to any location. Bring one along in a small, tight-wire carrier. If that doesn't pique your cat's curiosity, nothing will. Make sure that the cat doesn't have the opportunity to see the mouse or rat until the last minute.

Food reward is excellent with cats, but despite what the uninitiated think, they will work for petting, rubbing and scratching. Also, use feathers and other lures to attract the cat. A fly fisherman's equipment can work here. Make sure you remove the hook. We want to get the cat's attention, not a trout.

Clickers, buzzers and other noise makers are often used to train cats and other animals. I use verbal commands. Once when I was supplying the dogs for a film and someone else was supplying the cats, the director called for the cat and said, "Action!" The camera rolled but there was no cat. Without saying "Cut!" the director called "Action!" again and then, "Where's the cat? Action!" Complete silence, except for the expensive rolling of the camera. "Action!"—again with no action until the cat handler drawled, "I lost my damn clicker!" Now you know why I use verbal commands.

Remember, theatrical training should be a lifelong process.

# Motivating Your Pet

YOUNG ACTOR:
(*to director*):
"What is my
motivation?"

DIRECTOR: "You're
getting paid!"

We have dominion over the animals. This is an important point, particularly if you have exotic animals—those animals not usually kept as pets. The exotic animal owner has less competition in showBiz but more responsibilities. Generally more difficult to care for, the exotics are often not at home in your home. Their health, well-being, safety and care are your concern, however. Some exotics, such as big cats, can be dangerous to people, and that is an added responsibility. Dog and cat owners have similar responsibilities but not on the same scale, because these animals are not as difficult or potentially dangerous as exotics. Wild animals belong in the wild and it is not practical to domesticate them. *They are not domestic animals.* Once you have domesticated them, you are responsible for them for life. We must make a distinction between *dominion* and *domination. Dominion* comes from the Latin for "lord" or "master," stressing the master's responsibility. *Domination,* also from the Latin, means "rule or control," "despotism." Used with an animal, it implies that it's oppressed and under the gun. The animals are our responsibility but at the same time someone must be in charge, someone

67

who can make the best, most logical decisions. We have dominion, not domination over animals. For this reason we must motivate animals to do our bidding.

No, not training. *Motivating* your pet. Getting your pet to do what you want, in a fashion that is pleasurable and enjoyable for him. On occasion you must "make" your friend perform. You cannot have a film crew sitting on their rumps at thousands of dollars an hour while you plead your case with Tartuffe the Turkey. There are times when you want your pet to do it the first time every time. Remember in animal work to shoot rehearsals. As soon as the director says, "Let's rehearse the animal action," you say, "We *always* shoot rehearsals"—even if it is your first time on the set. The cost of that extra film is minuscule compared with what can be spent attempting to duplicate the perfect performance at rehearsal. Raw stock cost may seem astronomical to you, but film is the cheapest commodity on the set.

This short chapter is not meant to be a treatise on animal training and behavior. Not only is there insufficient space to cover the subject, but it is impossible to discuss the motivating factors for the many kinds of animals used in showBiz. A dolphin is not a dog, and a horse is not a hamster. As a matter of fact, a cat is not a cat and a dog is not a dog. If you are familiar with the behavior of dogs or cats, I would ask you to reflect on the difference in motivating a Siamese and Ragdoll cat or an Afghan Hound and Standard Poodle dog. Even the wags who refer to wolf and dog behavior as one are off base. Dogs have taught us more about wolves than wolves have told us about dogs. It is also more pleasant to work with a dog playing a wolf than a wolf playing a wolf.

There is the XYZ method of training animals and there is the ABC method. There are more "methods" of training dogs because there are so many dog trainers around. Very often, particularly when a person's name is connected with the method, it is not a method at all but merely a technique or a collection of techniques. A method has a philosophy that runs throughout the training or a part of the training. Many books have been written on training dogs. Read as many of them as possible. Howell Book House, my publisher, has an outstanding list.

An excellent starting book on general animal (and human) training is Karen Pryor's *Don't Shoot the Dog*. It will get you thinking. (Don't confuse it with Jackie Cooper's *Don't Shoot My Dog*, another interesting book that will give you showBiz insight into child actors.)

Food reward is a technique used in animal training. The use of food to create a single behavior (oh, how I hate that word) is a technique. If used in training the animal to do all or a lot of exercises, it is a method. A technique used in a single exercise does not a method make.

Why do I dislike the term *behavior* as compared to *exercise*? Behavior connotes conditioning and exercise connotes training. I'm an animal trainer. Pavlov was an animal conditioner. Conditioning is a science. Training is an art. In a scientific approach all reinforcement, positive and negative, is a prescribed amount. Dull, boring and exact. I prefer practicing the art of training, in which I continually consider who the animal is, its breed, its level of training, mood, attention, age, sex and time of day, and quickly respond with the appropriate reinforcement. It is done throughout the training session. Faster than a speeding computer, more powerful than a locomotive. I must analyze all of these factors and in a millisecond—no, a nanosecond—take the appropriate action. Man, that is an art!

# ★ SOME BASIC TRAINING PRINCIPLES

Let's discuss some basic principles for training animals. These remarks certainly apply to dogs and cats, which consist of 80 percent of showBiz animals. Later on I'll include more specific information about dogs and cats.

Training animals should involve a number of things. Fun, love, affection, rapport, understanding, respect, fairness, patience, repetition, setting a pattern and always letting your animal win. All of these items apply to both you and the animal. If training the animal is not fun for the animal *and* you, it is time to get out of the business. The business end is tough enough without both of you enjoying the training. You should love your work as much as your feathered or furry friend, and your friend should love you as much as you love it. If love is too strong a word for you, consider the word *affection.* If you have affection for your animal, it will love you. Animals that you train have an advantage over humans. Animals can see their god. From that mutual love/affection will develop a rapport and an understanding that will let the two of you work as one and turn in award-winning performances. They say the advantage of stage over film is that you can hear the audience's appreciation. That is not 100 percent true. Turn in that stellar performance in a studio setting and you will hear the approval of an applauding crew. Adulation from your peers is what really lets you know you have done a fine job.

Respect your animal's capabilities and limitations. Don't ask it to do anything that it can't. If you respect it, that respect will be returned. It is your job to be fair. You are controlling the situation. If you are unfair, it will be reflected in the animal's performance. You may be able to fool the general public but not your animal. It knows you too well. Have patience when training and working. ShowBiz is a hurry-up-and-wait business. You will have plenty of time to reread this book while you are waiting to be called. Don't become impatient with your friend. Training takes countless repetitions. If you become bored, stop the session. Do not permit yourself to lose your temper with your animal.

Once you have created enough repetitions of a particular exercise, you can start setting patterns to be followed by your animal. Your judicious jackdaw, "Jackie," will know it is training time by your behavior. The jackdaw, like other animals, benefits from rapport, understanding and love. Last, but not least, always let your animal win. Before you put the animal away, have it successfully complete the exercise with a rambunctious reward of praise.

Food reward is something that has been debated in dog-training circles for a long time. It sounds nice. Novices love to feed dogs. The experienced, competent, professional dog trainer does not advocate food reward as a method of training. I'm philosophically opposed to food reward. I think a good deal more of dogs than to use food reward. Dogs work better for praise than bribes. No, I don't "pay" them for their services. I praise them.

Your utmost concern is to get the dog to work. Nothing succeeds like success, and if food gets the dog to work, fine. It should be used as a backup technique rather than a dog-training philosophy. When you arrive on a film set, all stops are out. You should be willing to do whatever it takes to get your dog to do what it is supposed to do.

Now cat trainers, that's a horse of a different color. Cats will work for food reward, and it is more practical with cats than praise. But even though some misguided people think that food is the only way, do not underestimate the cat. As I said in the last chapter, food is not the only thing that will get cats to work. As a matter of fact, they are very, very fussy eaters, and it is difficult to tempt their palate, particularly when you have to. They are a highly tactile animal and will work for scratching and petting. Warmth also attracts them. In a film studio, there are all sorts of hot lights that a cat will enjoy curling up under.

Let's distinguish between training and handling. Training is teaching an animal to do an exercise. Handling is getting the animal to appear to do that exercise—even if the training has not been put in. If the training has been put in, so much the better and so much easier the job.

A good example of handling is mentioned in Ralph Helfer's *The Beauty of the Beasts*. Helfer was supplying the elk for the Hartford Insurance Company's TV commercial. The director wanted the elk, which is the Hartford's logo, to walk to a given high spot, look over the valley majestically and move on. Helfer had his men call the animal, named Lawrence (training) while they shook the feed bucket filled with Lawrence's favorite food (conditioning). When Lawrence reached the appropriate spot, one handler came rushing across to him, banging on a large piece of sheet metal (handling). Lawrence's reaction was to stop and look regally at the crazy commotion (handling). When the handler stopped banging the sheet metal, the handler with the feed bucket called Lawrence again (training) and rattled the bucket (conditioning) and Lawrence completed his journey.

Food reward has a couple of subheadings, which are not technically food reward: *luring* and *baiting*. Food reward is a technique used to train animals. The animal performs and you instantly give it a food reward. Luring is using food, or some other item, to attract an animal's attention and guide its movement. An example of luring would be a mouse in a small cage used to draw a cat's attention and movement forward. A mouse in a cage is an excellent device for attracting the attention of a number of different animals. Baiting is attracting the animal's attention with food and occasionally giving it a tidbit. The best example of this is seen at dog shows, where the handlers get their charges to stare alertly and rigidly at the food held in front of them. They are not allowed to snap at or grab the food, just freeze.

Once we had to do a Jim Dandy dog food commercial with a Saint Bernard. "The dog doesn't have to do anything," we were told, "just stand there." When we arrived on the sound stage we were told that the dog should push the Dutch door open, do a double take at the camera, walk down one side of the kitchen, sniff at this cabinet here, make a right turn here, sniff at this cabinet, make another right on the other side of the kitchen, put his paws up on the stool next to the counter and knock over a bag of oranges. A piece of cake.

"But what happened to the dog just standing there?" I asked.

"That'll come later."

We walked the dog through the kitchen a couple of times and then decided to give it a shot. I had a handler hidden behind the door and another handler behind the cabinet with the bag of oranges. I was behind the camera. The handler behind the door held the Saint in a standing position (handling). Rather than using a sit stay I prefer having a handler holding the dog back so we get a split-second start when the camera is ready. The dog is in gear and ready to come when called.

I called the dog (training). The handler behind the door nudged it open and released the dog (handling). I made a squeak and another squeak for the dog's double take (handling). The dog then moved down one side of the kitchen to sniff at the food placed behind the first cabinet door (luring). The moving of the dog through these positions in the kitchen was training (setting the pattern), shortly before the filming. The dog then turned and went to the second counter and sniffed (luring) the hidden food. The second handler behind the counter then called the dog and he came up to the counter (training). The dog followed the hand with the food while climbing up on the handler (luring) rather than the stool. His hand without the food was spread across the bottom of the Saint's rib cage and lifted the dog upward (handling). The hand with the food couldn't be seen by the camera as it was hidden behind the bag of oranges. With his finger, the handler tipped over the bag of oranges and had his hand disappear behind the counter. The dog stared at the food (baiting) left under the bag as he was told "Stay" (training). This gave the appearance of the dog looking down at the bag of oranges.

Incidentally, the camera only shows two dimensions, not three. That's why the position of the camera in relation to the animal can create many illusions. You will hear the expressions "cheat" and "cheating." This is not bad. It is good because the direction an animal is looking and the distance that an animal is from a prop or actor may not be correct, but it will appear to be correct on camera.

## ★ HOW TO GET DOGS AND CATS TO PERFORM

Let's consider some of the techniques used to get dogs and cats to perform. Cats are finicky eaters. Dogs that have been trained with a lot of food reward will develop the habit of eating. The pattern of eating has been set, and dogs will automatically take tidbits that they do not find particularly interesting. Eating becomes part of the dog's routine, unlike the case with the finicky cat. Dogs develop the *habit* of eating; cats usually do not. The most practical way to handle food for a cat is to use jars of baby food. Strained chicken is a cat favorite, and it is easy to handle. The small, wide-mouthed jar eliminates the need to touch the food, so it is not messy. It takes just a split second to twist it open and let the cat momentarily lick the inside of the jar. A cat can't grab hold of the entire jar as a dog might. This is an important factor. You don't want the animal to become satiated. Baby food is easy to control without premeasuring. And while baby food can work well for dogs, too, with dogs I prefer using American cheese slices separated by paper. A small piece of cheese, about half the size of a dime, can be carried in the anatomical snuff box (see the photographs between pages 50 and 51).

It takes a bit of speed and dexterity to replace the consumed cheese. The food should be held in the center of the palm, moved to the anatomical snuff box, and then dispensed with the thumb and forefinger. It takes practice. The food should be carried and dispensed from the one hand. If carried in two hands the keen nose of the dog will detect it and be distracted by the holding hand rather than focusing on the dispensing hand. Cheese is highly palatable to the dog but a little messy. If the dog has received a lot of food reward, small pellets of extruded dog food will make an excellent food reward, and it is not as messy. Also less messy than cheese is Liver Slivers, a commercial dog treat product. It is a good idea to have the food handy anytime you go to work. Always carry food in your theatrical bag, and beware of spoilage.

Know your animal and you will know how to motivate it. Mr. Cat is a great cat. If you tell him to get off the desk you are working on, he'll promptly ignore you. Use the "F-word" and he takes off like a shot. As in "Get the f——out of here!" He has to be properly motivated.

# VII

# What Animals Are Best for Show Business?

The animal that is best for show business is the one that you own. If you own an unusual animal, three things are going to happen. Let's assume you have a tapir. You will know more about tapirs than anyone else. You will not get too many calls for a tapir, but if the call goes out for a tapir you'll probably get the job. "But they are nocturnal," you say, "and they would be great for advertising a business that is open all night long." You know, and I know, and now the readers of this book know, that tapirs are nocturnal. The ad agency realizes that no one else knows that the tapir is nocturnal. In the ad for the business that is open all night long they are going to use an owl. Everyone knows that owls are nocturnal. "But tapirs are ungulates," you protest. I'm going to ask odd- or even-toed ungulate? Everyone else is going to ask, "What the hell is an ungulate?" "But the tapir is approaching extinction," you continue to protest, "and could be used in a PSA (public service announcement) dealing with protecting the environment." The advertising agency (if you ever get to talk to them) will explain that pandas are cuter. Let's face it, you are not going to get many calls, but as I said, if they do call you, you'll get the job.

A while ago an agency was using an *Our Gang*–type kid in a commercial and they wanted an *Our Gang* Petey–type of dog. The breed selected was a Bull Terrier, and I was to apply the characteristic eye-patch makeup. They were prudent enough to bring in all the kids they were considering for the commercial to see how they related to the dog. Great! Terrific preplanning! I loved the idea and was enthusiastic about the job.

Right before we were to shoot the commercial the agency called me and said that their legal department said they couldn't use a Petey-type dog. I explained that the *Our Gang* comedies had no lock on dogs with a patch over their eyes. I further explained that I had won a Bronze Medal at an Atlanta film festival for a Bull Terrier with a patch over his eye. Furthermore, the dog in the *Our Gang* comedies was not a Bull Terrier but an American (Pit) Bull Terrier. (This was before Pit Bulls got such bad press.) No one could argue with "Legal," and they wanted a Dalmatian. Now a Dalmatian is a much easier breed to get than a Bull Terrier and not a bad second choice, but it was not 100 percent right. A Bull Terrier or a Pit Bull were right on. I was crestfallen. I wanted to do the commercial badly—but with the right breed, a Bull Terrier, not a Dalmatian. I told them I couldn't get a Dalmatian and gracefully bowed out.

You can tell when a commercial or a film you are working on has that measure of greatness. I had that feeling with this commercial, if they used a Bull Terrier. Sometime later I talked to that marvelous character actor Malachy McCourt, who was playing the grocer in that commercial. I asked him how the commercial did. Actors know how well a commercial does by the amount of residuals they receive. He told me it bombed. I was right. Still not President, but right!

No matter what animal you have, no matter what breed you have, there is a commercial for everyone. Andy Warhol's *aperçu* that everyone will be famous for fifteen minutes also applies to animals.

# ★ THE BEST SHOW BUSINESS ANIMALS (WITH THE EMPHASIS ON DOGS)

Mutts are asked for most often, but I do not like to supply mutts. First, I don't like the term "mutt." I prefer "generic dog" or "random-bred dog." It has more class! The reason I don't like to use random-bred dogs is they are impossible to match. I remember receiving a call for a generic dog for a tire commercial. My recommendation was to go with a purebred dog that looks like a generic dog. The man from the ad agency was offended. It was a single commercial, and they just needed one dog. We were off on the wrong foot. I would rather bow out than become involved in a friction-filled job. I had apparently overstepped my bounds with my recommendation.

About six months later I received a call from a man who was trying to match a dog. He was giving me measurements that I knew were wrong. The average person cannot properly measure a dog. Furthermore, that is not the way to match dogs. As the conversation developed and we discussed the commercial, I realized that this was the same advertising campaign I had been called about six months earlier. I bluntly told him that I had cautioned him about the problems in matching a random-bred dog. He said that this was the first time they were using a dog in a commercial and denied any previous involvement. If so, why did he want to match the dog? Not only was this the same campaign but the same person I had talked to six months before—and his brusque termination of the phone call proved that fact.

I recall talking to a customer about how I turned down these jobs. I felt it was a question of ethics. She said that I had an ulterior and monetary motive. I was offended, but she quickly explained how I saved a fortune in psychological counseling. Like Samuel Goldwyn said, "Anyone who goes to a psychiatrist ought to have his head examined."

A medium-sized, broken-coated generic dog either in light shades of brown or gray is the perfect pup for show Business. Good for all jobs? No, but this is the most asked-for type of dog. While fashions in advertising and film change, the dog from Middle America has been with us a long time, and well it should. Everyone seems to own a medium-sized dog. A wire or long coat photographs much better than a smooth coat; there are all sorts of highlights and gradations in the coat that make the dog easier to read and more pleasing to view. And brown or tan is the preferred color. On the cat side, an orange tabby would qualify here.

If we were to shoot a black cat or black Doberman sleeping it would look like a black blob. You would never use a Doberman in a commercial because they have the image of being too fierce. The same is true of the German Shepherd. At one time I was able to say that I never supplied a Shepherd or a Dobe for a commercial. Then I shot two commercials on the same day—one with a Shepherd and the other with two Dobes. Since then I have not supplied either breed for a commercial, nor have I even received a query. These breeds are great when someone wants a movie with a fierce dog, but they just have no appeal in commercials.

The interesting thing about the Shepherd and the Dobes was that one commercial was being shot for Japan and the other for Germany. The German commercial took place under the Brooklyn Bridge with New York City's famous skyline in the background. The scene was supposed to be an auto chop shop operated by nefarious characters and protected by guard dogs. Then the police move in and bust the place. The tag line of the commercial (in German, of course) was "The Volkswagen Rabbit. The most frequently stolen car in America." That commercial was definitely not for U.S. viewing.

What is the best breed of dog? There is no *best* breed. Different jobs require different breeds. Let's talk about fashion modeling and high-fashion models. High-fashion models are those tall, anorexic, high-cheekboned, ethereal creatures who walk with their pelvis thrust forward slightly, as if they were walking up a hill. You can shoot a high-fashion model in an evening gown, a business suit or in tweeds. Same model, different outfits. Not only different outfits but different messages are being conveyed.

The evening gown requires a breed as anorexic as the model. If it were an interior shot or on a lawn in front of the manor, my choice would be a Borzoi. The sleek Borzoi conveys style, class, grace, money. With that evening gown and diamonds, a Borzoi is a girl's best friend. If I were to go with exotic animals my choice in this setting would be a black leopard. For a domestic cat, my choice would be a Siamese or Abyssinian.

Wolfschmidt vodka ran a series of very successful print jobs utilizing the Borzoi. The ads were period pieces of the Czar and Czarina. Definitely upscale! An interesting point in the Wolfschmidt ad was the Borzoi's popular name, Russian Wolfhound, which tied in well with the brand name. If the model were not in front of a manor house or villa but instead on a hill with an Arabian horse off in the background, some might be tempted to use an Afghan Hound. Wrong! It should be a Saluki.

I would never permit a Borzoi to be used in a Wolfschmidt ad in England because there is an English brand of vodka called Borzoi. A conflicting or competing image is an important factor in advertising. A once-popular breed of dog that worked out well for dog food commercials was the

Collie. Collies were dead in the water when Recipe dog food was introduced, with Lassie and her late, great trainer, Rudd Weatherwax, as spokesdog and spokesperson for the product. No self-respecting advertising agency would permit the use of a Collie or Shetland Sheepdog (a Collie in miniature) in their dog food advertising. To illustrate the power of the Lassie image, this dog food product was introduced to the market and overnight became one of the top five canned foods.

Once we put our high-fashion model in a business suit, we need a different dog. I would go for the Standard Manchester Terrier, a smooth-coated, black and tan dog that looks like a small (twenty-two pounds or less) Doberman with a tail. That breed is all business, with a bright, alert, sleek and sharp look. If the ad were for a clothing line trying to convey the image of an aggressive businesswoman I *might* go to the Doberman Pinscher, which could be risky because of its aggressive image. I would use the red, blue or fawn-colored Dobe rather than the black for this advertisement. Those colors photograph softer and better than the black. My prime choice would be the rarer Isabella (fawn). Another choice would be the Boston Terrier; it's sleek but not slim, with an all-business attitude and aggression indicated by the bulldog-type head. The so-called hand-painted Boston takes on a tuxedo appearance, adding to the upscale look.

Any terrier can indicate all-business, but once we get into the broken-coated terriers, a softness appears. A Smooth Fox Terrier might be acceptable, but if the Wire Fox Terrier were used it would have to be immaculately plucked and trimmed with no hair out of place. Once I got into a protracted discussion with an advertising agency that wanted a print ad with an elegant dog behind the tall wrought-iron gate of a palatial estate and with a scruffy dog on the outside to show a rich dog, poor dog theme. We couldn't agree on breeds and I bowed out. They wanted to

use two Wire Fox Terriers. The one inside was professionally groomed and the one outside had a scruffy appearance.
This approach would only be viable if they wanted to make
a very strong point that the dog on the outside was a poor
relative. That was not the point of the advertisement. Their
solution was interesting, but not one that I would have
chosen. (*Note:* Once you have agreed to do a job you have
a moral obligation to complete the job to the best of your
ability. Even if there is a major change in the job, you have
that obligation unless in your heart of hearts you know it
is wrong or dangerous. Your responsibility for keeping the
animal out of danger is greater than self-protection. Danger
to the animal is the ultimate reason to refuse.) Advertising
agencies are foolish if they do not take advantage of the
expertise of those supplying them animals regarding the
subtle images that are created in an ad. An ad becomes less
than the sum of all its parts if input from the experts is
ignored.

The cat for the high-fashion model in a business suit is
the Balinese—with the exotic animal, a panther.

Now Miss High Fashion Model is wearing a tweed
outfit. Where do we want to shoot this? Outdoors in a fall
setting with an Irish Setter. (Fall settings are shot in the
summertime, about three seasons too late. Prop houses
will sell you a large garbage bag of last year's fallen leaves
for about $75 to $100. And you have been burning them!)
The Irish Setter is a high-fashion, sporty dog. The Irish
Setter we select should be the beautiful show type and not
the field-type Red Setter that is used for hunting. High
fashion is the appearance of hunting and not hunting itself.
The only true hunting background we could have would be
with a group of Foxhounds and everyone on horseback
would be garbed in the traditional costume rather than
tweed. In the United States it is virtually impossible to
photograph this sort of scene. One of the tenets of the
Masters of Foxhounds Association of America is that mem-

bers may *not* use their hounds for commercial advertising purposes. Members of this association have so much money that there is nothing you can offer them that will permit them to sell out the association. Each member seems to have more money than God. If you are stuck getting a pack of hounds, give me a call. I have a solution or two that doesn't require a trip to merry old England.

On the cat side for the tweed look, I would suggest the Havana Brown. In exotics I would go for a falcon or golden eagle.

The above is not a complete treatise on the subject, but it is designed to get you thinking along the right lines. If you have one animal you are working with, that is the best one for the job. You have no obligation to advise the ad agency. The full-fledged "animal agency" or "animal renter" does have this obligation, although they are not required to do a job if they feel the animal is wrong.

# Images Created by Animals

"You can't depend on your eyes when your imagination is out of focus."

Mark Twain

Animals are not negative. They are positive. Even a low-down sidewinder, a rattler, can present a positive image with the right tagline. Before the Stars and Stripes, many southern states used a rattlesnake on their flag. The negative motto presented a positive position: "Don't Tread On Me." This snake was particularly appropriate because it has thirteen rattles and the species *Crotalus* is indigenous to the United States (with some in Canada and Mexico). The South and Southwest are where most of them hang out.

The morning's radio tells the story of a TV star arrested on drug and weapons charges. There is no such problem with animals. Studio contracts in the old Hollywood days contained a morals clause. It was never necessary to put that clause in a contract with Rhubarb, Lassie or Rin-Tin-Tin, much to the joy of advertisers. Today it is hard to determine just what is scandalous conduct, but it is always a concern to those on Madison Avenue. Another advantage of animals is the money saved in makeup fees.

You are embarking on a journey that is the true American Dream: starting off with little or no cash and hopefully steamrolling into a lucrative, glamorous business. But remember, the Declaration of Independence doesn't guarantee happiness. It guarantees the *pursuit* of happiness. You can go into many different directions in your pursuit, so get started.

You have to be out there plugging the use of animals in general, and your animal specifically. Don't worry about human actors losing their jobs to animals. Look how many animal actors the musical *Cats* put out of work.

Now, when we talk about animals, we are talking about an uncountable number of organisms—multicelled, organized into tissue—that ingest food. Man, that's a lot of organisms—and you may be called on to supply any one of them!

Should you want to start your own animal agency, you should have at your disposal at least one each of the following: bear, elephant, lion and chimp. They are the four most used exotic animals. Make sure that you also have someone with a lot of experience in handling them. Each one requires specialized techniques.

The strong images created by animals—from Merrill Lynch's broad, bustling bull to RCA's diminutive Parson Jack Russell Terrier—have made them the darlings of the advertising industry. They have truly sold products over the years. The majestic lion is used by both MGM and Dreyfus. The messages are hard sell and subtle. Merrill Lynch's bull is powerful and aggressive, suggesting a bull market over a bear market. The picture of a terrier listening to "His Master's Voice" on an old Victrola has been around longer than the vast majority of the people buying RCA's products. That is the subtle, understated sell. The King of Beasts represents both an ever-expanding entertainment company and an investment firm.

It is impossible to list the images conveyed by every animal alive, but exotic animals, by their very nature, convey specific images. If we want to suggest mountainous power and strength, what finer animal could we use than the towering bear. While seemingly contradictory, the bear also conveys a quiet patience through its Wall Street image of a bear market. A bear market is a sleeping giant, waiting to be awakened from its hibernation. Merrill Lynch successfully uses the bull to demonstrate the aggressive power and strength of the stock market and that firm's approach to it. Here we have two different animals demonstrating power, size, and strength but *different* kinds of power, size, and strength. One is rested and reserved, while the other is moving and forceful. The bull-in-a-china-shop image immediately changes the picture to one of clumsy, ruthless, destructive power.

To convey ultimate size we have the gargantuan land-bound elephant and the water-bound whale. The much-used whale of a sale in a modest ad campaign conveys gigantic savings.

All positive images.

Now to the images conveyed by the various breeds of dogs and cats.


# ★ DOGS

Dogs play an extremely important part in our culture. Some dog images can arouse conflicting feelings, even within the same person. We respond to subliminal cues. One of the factors that affects these impressions is the age of the targeted audience. People who came of age in the thirties and forties know what a Boston Terrier is, while those who came of age in the fifties and sixties think that it is a miniature Boxer. The children of the seventies confuse the Boxer with the Bull Mastiff and those of the eighties and nineties subliminally think of the Bull Mastiff as a brown Rottweiler.

Remember, the advantage of using a purebred dog over a random-bred dog is that it is easier to match. A great plus is the breed that doesn't look like a purebred.

Advertising has identified the Bulldog with the Mack truck, as in "Built like a Mack," and the Jack Russell Terrier and/or Smooth Fox Terrier with "His Master's Voice" for RCA Victor, Tigue for Buster Brown shoes and the Cocker Spaniel for Coppertone. An excellent article for the research-minded is Mordecai Siegal's "Dogs of Madison Avenue" in the April 1976 *Pure-bred Dogs/American Kennel Gazette.*

While people may not know a dog's breed, they are aware of the images it creates—many of which are not true. For example, the Irish Wolfhound conveys the impression of an ancient breed that hunted wolves. In reality, the breed was reconstituted in the early part of the nineteenth century when Ireland was devoid of wolves. It is not only commercials that rely on breed images. A character in a play or feature film can be rapidly defined by the type of dog he or she owns.

What follows is not an attempt to describe the physical appearance of the various breeds but rather to provide thumbnail sketches of the images they create and an occasional recommendation as to the role product the dog could enhance.

## Sporting Dogs

All of the sporting dog breeds naturally convey a sporty, outdoor image.

**BRITTANY**  Bright, active, nondescript, Everyman's dog. Being a generic or brand "X" dog is an asset for the showBiz dog.

**GERMAN SHORTHAIRED POINTER**  A popular breed, used extensively for hunting birds. A generic all-around hunter.

**GERMAN WIREHAIRED POINTER**   Even more generic than the Shorthair. This breed with its broken coat will photograph better and "muttier."

**CHESAPEAKE BAY RETRIEVER**   American. Rough and ready. Rambunctious tough guy. Hard charging, all weather. Historical. Chesapeake Bay area. This breed could be the spokesdog for an "early American" food product such as country-smoked duck or turkey.

**CURLY-COATED RETRIEVER**   Photographs better than the Flat-Coated Retriever because of the texture of the tight curly coat. Unique, tough, but not quite a generic dog.

**FLAT-COATED RETRIEVER**   Reserved, upscale, calm and appears to be a random-bred dog.

**GOLDEN RETRIEVER**   Friendly, fun loving, lover of children. Originally popularized in advertising because of its generic look, it became extremely recognizable. It still has the connotation of Everyman's dog. Color, coat texture and tractability make it a perennial favorite for ads and commercials. An excellent spokesdog for a dog food because of its size and happy, outgoing nature. Tests have shown that dog owners feel that their dogs are larger than they actually are, which causes dog food companies to use larger dogs. Larger dogs consume more dog food, also desired by the dog food company.

**LABRADOR RETRIEVER**   Excellent image as a sporty, outdoor, rough-and-ready, active hunting dog. The yellow photographs best, followed by the liver and then the black, which takes on an ominous look. Tweedy.

**ENGLISH SETTER**   Upscale, sedate, refined hunting dog. Boots and jodhpurs rather than tweeds. English.

**GORDON SETTER**   Scottish. Calm, upscale, reserved. An upscale brand of Scotch whisky would handily profit from a Gordon Setter as spokesdog.

**IRISH SETTER**   Fast, flashy, active, upscale. The most recognizable of the Setters.

**AMERICAN WATER SPANIEL**   Nondescript, random-bred pet. All-American. Compact.

**CLUMBER SPANIEL**   Unique. Slow. Overweight.

**AMERICAN COCKER SPANIEL**   Popular, active, merry. Nasty, aggressive. Pet. Show dog. American. Purebred.

**ENGLISH COCKER SPANIEL**   Fun, pleasant, active. Less defined than the American Cocker and somewhat less purebred.

**ENGLISH SPRINGER SPANIEL**   Fun, friendly, active hunter. Aggressive, tough, fast. Not quite blue-collar.

**FIELD SPANIEL**   Nondescript hunting spaniel. Not purebred. Friendly pet.

**IRISH WATER SPANIEL**   Clown, fun loving, wild, playful, nondescript. Irish.

**SUSSEX SPANIEL**   Happy, random bred.

**WELSH SPRINGER SPANIEL**   Slightly upscale, not easily identifiable. Happy, outgoing, active.

**VIZSLA**   Sleek, placid, affectionate. Readily identified as a hunting dog but difficult to identify the type of quarry.

**WEIMARANER**   Gray ghost. Definite hunting dog. Ethereal. Fast, active.

**WIREHAIRED POINTING GRIFFON**   Random-bred hunting dog whose quarry is difficult to identify. Cute. Active.

## Hounds

Hounds are divided into two general families: the trail hound (nose to the ground tracking its quarry) and the sight hound (Greyhound). The two notable exceptions—which, in truth, do not belong to either classification—are the Basenji and the Norwegian Elkhound. Most trail hounds, with the exception of Foxhounds and Harriers, take on the connotation of pickup truck, rifle in the back window rack. Greyhounds are thin, elegant and upscale. As Coco Chanel said, you can't be too rich or too thin.

**AFGHAN HOUND** Upscale, elegant, refined, sleek. Horsey. Foreign, Mid-East, Afghanistan. Plains and mountains. Swift. Catlike. An excellent image for a firm selling higher-priced, native-made Afghan blankets.

**BASENJI** Quiet, no barking, African. Not easily identified as to actual breed but is recognizable as a purebred. This recognition as a purebred automatically increases the perceived value of the product, thus making the silent Basenji a spokesdog (using ASL, or American Sign Language). It would be an added advantage if a targeted audience was African-American.

**BASSETT HOUND** Cute, cuddly. Hush Puppy shoes. Comical, funny, sense of humor. French. Southern redneck.

**BEAGLE** Rabbit hound. Cute, friendly, readily recognizable as a purebred but still has the look of a random bred.

**BLACK AND TAN COONHOUND** Blue collar, good ole boy. American, southern. Slow, lazy, lounging around. Raccoon hunter.

**BLOODHOUND** Vicious tracker of slaves and prisoners. Great nose, ability to identify odors. A tenacious pursuer. Endurance. Staying power. An excellent spokesdog for deodorants and odor killers, particularly those wishing to stress long duration. American (although the breed is not). Redneck southern hunting, lazy, slow.

**BORZOI** Russian Wolfhound. Troika. Swift, sleek, anorexic. Ultra high-fashion shots. Elegant, expensive, exclusive. The most upscale. Royalty, further emphasized by the Wolfschmidt vodka series of ads.

**DACHSHUND** Frankfurter dog. Hot dog. Germanic. Long. Beer and schnapps. Cute and friendly. Pet that can be simultaneously petted by a large family.

**AMERICAN FOXHOUND** American. English. Upscale. Hunting as a refined, cultured sport. Proper.

**ENGLISH FOXHOUND** Hunting in packs. Horsey. English. Refined, cultured, social, proper, upscale, gentlemanly. Old school ties.

**GREYHOUND** Sleek, swift, racing. Graceful, upscale. Buses. Anorexic. The ultimate in speed. The spokesdog for Greyhound bus lines.

**HARRIER** A smaller version of the two Foxhounds. In a pack they can become a substitute for Foxhounds, which are nearly impossible to photograph for commercial purposes. When people have everything, what can you give them to entice them to commercialize their Foxhounds? Filthy lucre is only filthy to those with unlimited supplies.

**IBIZAN HOUND** Elegant, graceful, upscale. Contradicts their status as stray dogs in Spain, where I first saw them in the late fifties. Thin. Spanish. Swift.

**IRISH WOLFHOUND** Enormous. Irish. Huge but graceful. Fast rather than swift. Ancient, old. Dependable. Docile. Fierce hunter of wolves. Regal. Royal. A great spokesdog for an upscale cleaning product that is really tough on dirt. If the product has an Irish name or was manufactured in Ireland, so much the better.

**NORWEGIAN ELKHOUND**  Norwegian, compact. Pet rather than a hunter. Good watch dog.

**OTTER HOUND**  A great breed for the feature film wanting a large "shaggy dog." Cute. Frightening. Ferocious.

**PETIT BASSET GRIFFON VENDÉEN**  Cute, cuddly, comical. French.

**PHARAOH HOUND**  Sleek, elegant, graceful, upscale.

**RHODESIAN RIDGEBACK**  Rough, hard, tough, rugged. A hunter of lions. Africa. No nonsense. Guardian and protector.

**SALUKI**  Lithe, graceful, upscale. Horsey. Mountains and plains. Swift, fast, agile.

**SCOTTISH DEERHOUND**  Scotland. Speed and grace. Large size.

**WHIPPET**  Swift, agile, speedy. Compact, economical. Ancient. Dependable. What a great logo for a rush printing firm! A whippet standing in front of some hieroglyphics, perhaps spelling out the firm name.

## Working Dogs

Working dogs purportedly work for a living. They are not white-collar workers but rather draft animals and guardians.

**AKITA**  Japan. Large and powerful. Aggressive watch dog. Fighting dog. Inscrutable. I made the "inscrutable" remark in an often quoted *Sports Illustrated* article. One Akita fancier wrote a letter to an Akita magazine taking exception to it. From the wording of the letter it was apparent that he didn't know what the word meant. He was nisei.

**ALASKAN MALAMUTE** Large, powerful sled dog. Used for pulling heavy loads. Freighter or carrier of heavy burdens by pack. Power and strength rather than speed. Alaska. Snow. Cold weather. What a logo for a large powerful four-wheeler that easily traverses the deepest snow!

**BERNESE MOUNTAIN DOG** Swiss. Large and powerful. Non-descript. A great larger mutt.

**BOXER** German. Fighter. Fast and playful. Powerful. Coiled strength and speed. Protector.

**BULL MASTIFF** Huge, powerful, strong guard dog. Security. Dependability.

**DOBERMAN PINSCHER** Aggressive. Vicious. Fast. Sharp. This breed would *never* be used in a commercial but would be a prime choice for a film depicting a dangerous situation requiring nasty, aggressive dogs. All business.

**GIANT SCHNAUZER** An oversized Miniature Schnauzer. Large, powerful, agile guard dog.

**GREAT DANE** German. Danish. Extremely large, towering, majestic, magnificent, powerful, grand. Elegant and Apollo-like. Handsome rather than pretty, even the females. Powerful and strong. Tall. Upscale. The moving firm Dane and Murphy successfully uses a cartoon of a Dane to suggest, in an elegant but humorous fashion, that they can move large and heavy loads.

**GREAT PYRENEES** France. Pyrenees Mountains. Spain. Large, powerful, mountainous and pure. Clean. A cleaning product that is used for heavy-duty cleaning and is economically priced would do well to consider this breed in their ad campaign. A Spanish or French designer bottled water firm could exploit this breed's image.

**KOMONDOR**  Massive guard dog. Livestock-guarding dog. Large, powerful and aggressive. Hungarian. The ultimate protector. Rastafarian. Dreadlocks.

**KUVASZ**  Hungarian. Large, powerful, pure, dependable, hard-charging guard dog. Livestock-guarding dog. Neat and clean.

**MASTIFF**  Upscale. Expensive. Ancient breed. Huge, mountainous, gigantic, mammoth, outsize, powerful, aggressive guard dog and protector.

**NEWFOUNDLAND**  Big, huge, gigantic, massive. Gentle giants. Black (although they come in other colors). Water rescue dogs. Safe, dependable, guardians of children. Here is a breed that illustrates the far-reaching results of our earliest imprinting regarding dogs. Most people do not know the name of this breed, but when they see a picture of the dog, all the above points seep into their minds. One color, the Landseer (a particolor), is named after the nineteenth-century English painter, who painted pictures of dogs that color. The most famous, "Saved," was of a Landseer rescuing a small child from drowning. Teddy bear.

**PORTUGUESE WATER DOG**  Foppish. Poodle-like. Clown. Water dog. Great swimmer. Playful, fun dog.

**ROTTWEILER**  Massive, forceful, mighty, enormous. Rough, tough, powerful and aggressive. Damian. The quintessential guard dog. A killer. Vicious. Dangerous. Not the breed for a commercial unless used to illustrate an indestructible, heavy-duty tire that was purchased primarily by the individual truck owner rather than the fleet owner.

**SAINT BERNARD**  Safe, dependable, religious, massive guardian of children. Safe travel. Larger than life. Snow. Alpine. Cold. Winter. Rescuer of travelers in the Alps. Brandy and brandy casks. A spokesdog for the responsible consumption of booze, particularly on a cold winter night before beginning your journey homeward, transported by a designated driver. Christian Brothers brandy, sign this breed up!

**SAMOYED**  Cold, snow, winter. Nordic. Russia. Siberia. Winter and white wastelands of snow. Sled dog. Purity. Whiteness. Clean. Teddy bear.

**SIBERIAN HUSKY**  Bitter cold, frigid, snow, winter. Siberia. Sled dog. Fast. Endurance. Cold starts. A racer rather than a freighter. Great for advertising an engine lubricant, such as Bonded Oil did to stress fast cold-winter starts.

**STANDARD SCHNAUZER**  Steady, dependable, rugged, tough, trim, well groomed. Excellent breed for a science fiction film in which a dog's size is increased or diminished via using the Giant and Miniature Schnauzer. While not related and not exact in appearance, the correct grooming would make it work.

## Herding

Herding breeds were developed to herd livestock. The image of a protector of the flock underlies every other image created. If the protected flock is sheep, this softens the image of the protector.

**AUSTRALIAN SHEPHERD**  Australia. Nondescript generic dog. Sheep. Intelligent, quick.

**AUSTRALIAN CATTLE DOG**  Australia. Rough, tough, with a rag-tag look. Rugged, dependable protector. Sensitive.

**BEARDED COLLIE**  Random-bred look. Excellent shaggy dog. Kid's dog. Farm dog. Pet, nondescript.

**BELGIAN MALINOIS**  Police dog. German Shepherd–type generic dog. Watch dog. Protector. Fast, agile, athletic. French. Belgian. Dutch. Flemish.

**BELGIAN SHEEPDOG**   Black, ominous, vicious, tough, fast, agile. Cuddly. Affectionate. Protector. Flemish. Dutch. French. Belgian.

**BELGIAN TERVUREN**   Cuddly, strong, affectionate, powerful, fast protector. Belgian. French. Dutch. Flemish.

**BOUVIER DES FLANDRES**   Big, powerful. A great massive shaggy dog. French. Belgian. Guardian. Watch dog.

**BRIARD**   A terrific, large shaggy dog. Sweet, affectionate, cuddly. Cheese. Guardian. A great imprint for a brand of Brie that rabidly guards its freshness in storing, packaging and shipping its product.

**ROUGH COLLIE**   Lassie. Scotland. Sheep. Superdog that can do anything. Loyal, dependable, placid, calm, all seeing, all knowing. Protector of the house and hearth.

**SMOOTH COLLIE**   No Collie images are conveyed by the smooth variety. Swift, fast, agile, unidentifiable.

**GERMAN SHEPHERD DOG**   Police dog. Watch dog. Attack dog. Guard dog. Vicious. German. Nazis. Military. Waffen SS. Sheep-herding dog. Another superdog that can do everything and actually does. Never to be used in commercials. Gravy Train dog food tried using this breed many years ago. It was a terrific campaign. The German Shepherd would perform some heroic deed and then jump on an old-fashioned locomotive pulling flatbed cars piled high with bags of Gravy Train. The Shepherd, after the superdog rescue, would stand proudly on the bags of dog food, and the tag line was, "Makes your dog feel like Rin-Tin-Tin." Great concept. Unbelievably good program. It didn't sell dog food. You can bring Rin-Tin-Tin into your house on a half-hour TV program, but not in a commercial. Commercial dogs have to be cute and friendly.

**OLD ENGLISH SHEEPDOG**  Shaggy dog. Large. English. Cute and cuddly. Ancient, dependable. This is a breed that was popularized by Madison Avenue. They were used so often for their then-undeterminable look that they became a very popular breed. I claim credit for popularizing the breed with the commercials and print jobs that I did.

**PULI**  Hungary. Compact, agile, fast. Dreadlocks.

**SHETLAND SHEEPDOG**  Miniature Collie. Lassie. Small superdog. Scotland. Sheep.

**CARDIGAN WELSH CORGI**  Cute, funny, affectionate. Half a dog high and two dogs long. Substantial. Solid. Wales.

**PEMBROKE WELSH CORGI**  Clown. Fun dog. Lovable. Welsh. A short dog for a long family. Hardy. Dependable.

## Terriers

Terriers are tough and resilient. They have a deserved reputation for being scrappers. This may seem like a negative image but it is not. It translates into hardness, toughness and durability. New images can be created with imaginative grooming.

**AIREDALE**  Pet. Police dog. Fast, smart, intelligent. England. Tall and stately.

**AMERICAN STAFFORDSHIRE**  Pit dog, fighter, scrapper, dangerous. American. Rough, tough, durable, endurance, staying power. *Little Rascals.* America in the twenties and thirties.

**AUSTRALIAN TERRIER**  Australia. Cute, funny, spunky.

**BEDLINGTON**  Little Bo Peep. Sheeplike. Cuddly, affectionate. Purity.

**BORDER TERRIER** Cute, comical, fun loving. Nondescript generic dog type.

**BULL TERRIER** Fighter, scrappy, tough, dangerous, pit dog. Purity (in the white variety). Staying power, endurance, tough, rough. *Our Gang*. Petey. Pugnacious.

**CAIRN** Scotland. Cute, funny, rough and tough. Cuddly. The quintessential mutt. Fast, rapid moving, active.

**DANDIE DINMONT** Cute, comical. Scotland. Guy Mannering. Generic dog type.

**FOX TERRIER (SMOOTH)** Crisp, clean, sharp, fast. Tough, scrappy.

**FOX TERRIER (WIRE)** Pristine, well groomed, sharp, crisp. Ungroomed, the dog has a random-bred dog quality to it. Bright, swift.

**IRISH TERRIER** Ireland. Rough, tough, scrappy, ready to fight. Crisp, alert, smart, fast. Red.

**KERRY BLUE** Irish. Blue. Aggressive, fast, scrappy, endurance, hardy.

**LAKELAND** Trim, sharp appearing, businesslike, alert, curious, quick.

**MANCHESTER TERRIER (STANDARD)** Alert, keen, tough, all business, aggressive, thorough, persistent.

**MINIATURE BULL TERRIER** Petey in *Our Gang*. Pit dog, fighter, smaller, compact, tough package. Aggressive, dangerous.

**MINIATURE SCHNAUZER** Yappy, quick, somewhat foppish. German. Low-end upscale. Can be immaculately and artfully groomed.

**NORWICH TERRIER** Feisty, quick, sharp, alert, scrappy. Cute. Playful pet. Smart.

**NORFOLK TERRIER**   Playful. Pet. Cuddly. Scrappy.

**SCOTTISH TERRIER**   Black & White whiskey has success-fully utilized this breed as one half of its logo. Scotland. Austere, tough, smart. All business.

**SEALYHAM**   Sweet, cute. Tough. Pure. Cock of the walk.

**SKYE**   Beautiful, graceful, placid. Scrappy, tough. Quick.

**SOFT-COATED WHEATEN**   Irish. Tough, feisty, willing to fight. Neat and trim.

**STAFFORDSHIRE BULL TERRIER**   Buster Brown shoes has made the breed famous by having Buster and the dog in their logo.

**WELSH TERRIER**   Welsh. Miniature Airedale. Neat, trim, slick, fast, alert. Upscale. A gentleman.

**WEST HIGHLAND WHITE TERRIER**   The other half of the Black & White whiskey logo. Purity. Fun loving, prankster, play-ful. Feisty, scrappy. Cute and cuddly.


## Toys

The tiniest of breeds, the Toys present an upscale, spoiled, yappy and catered-to image. Silk cushions, small size and gourmet dog food.

**AFFENPINSCHER**   Monkeylike. Very cute. Expressive. Alert. Fun loving, playful. Rugged.

**BRUSSELS GRIFFON**   Cute and cuddly. Sweet, affectionate, expressive. Hardy. Belgium.

**CHIHUAHUA**   Teeny tiny. The smallest of breeds. A great spokesdog for someone attempting to stress tiny and deli-cate miniaturization. Mexico. Sombreros, tequila, siestas. Yappy.

**CHINESE CRESTED** Unique, rarity. Delicate, sensitive. Hairless, bald. Mottled. Hot to the touch. Warm. Repulsive. Cute.

**ENGLISH TOY SPANIEL** Cute, comical, sweet, sturdy, affectionate. Nineteenth century.

**ITALIAN GREYHOUND** Very delicate. Tiny. Petite. Fast, rapid, speedy. Sensitive. Catlike. Lounge around. Italy. Ancient, fine. A firm specializing in the rapid repair of delicate china and porcelain or Italian jewelry would be wise to use an Italian Greyhound in its ad campaign.

**JAPANESE CHIN** Japan. Pet. Rugged. Affectionate.

**MALTESE** Prim, perfect, pure, delicate, sweet. Upscale, expensive.

**MANCHESTER TERRIER (TOY)** Sharp, businesslike, trim, squared away, aggressive, tough, rugged, small, tiny.

**MINIATURE PINSCHER** Petite Doberman. Sharp, fast, aggressive, trim, all business.

**PAPILLON** French. Butterfly, moth. Extremely alert. Delicate, small. Playful, affectionate.

**PEKINGESE** China, Beijing, Orient. Lion. Temple guard. Sleeve dog. Cute. Expressive. Rough and tough.

**POMERANIAN** Spitz. Alert. Petite, miniaturization. A great dog for a science fiction film depicting the growth or decrease in size of a dog.

**POODLE (TOY)** Petite. Elegant, upscale. Sissified, foppish. The spoiled dog of an extremely wealthy dowager. Yappy.

**PUG** Holland. Dutch. The nineties. Wealthy. Upscale. Husky, hefty, chunky. This would be a great breed to illustrate a small or miniature model of a Hefty bag.

**SHIH TZU**   Tibet. China. Oriental. Spoiled. Upscale, expensive.

**SILKY TERRIER**   Australia. Sydney. Nondescript Yorkshire Terrier type. Pet.

**YORKSHIRE TERRIER**   Small, yappy, upscale. Cute, spoiled, expensive.

## Nonsporting

This catch-all group of dogs suffers from the "Nonsporting" appellation putting them in the "Ornamental Dog" category. The English term "Utility Dogs" is superior to its American equivalent.

**BICHON FRISE**   White, pure, neat and clean. Cute and cuddly.

**BOSTON TERRIER**   America's gentleman. The nineties. Tuxedo. Neat, trim, sharp, well groomed. Pit dog. Black and white.

**BULLDOG**   English manqué. Churchill. Rough, tough. Stodgy. Broad, hefty, chunky, squat. Rolling gait, sea legs. Cigar smoking.

**CHINESE SHAR PEI**   Wrinkled. Funny looking. A forty-five-pound dog in a sixty-five-pound coat. Expensive, fancy. Unique, rare.

**CHOW CHOW**   Orient, China. The cutest puppies in the world. Round, fluffy, cuddly. Nasty, aggressive, vicious. Rugged, tough, rough. Palace guard dog.

**DALMATIAN**   Firehouse dog. Black and white. Spots. Pet. Highly recognized breed.

**FINNISH SPITZ**   Nordic sled dog. Generic dog.

**FRENCH BULLDOG** France, England. Rugged. Aggressive. When Bob Lilly was doing a commercial that required a Bulldog for Black & Decker, there were very specific size requirements for the dog because the dog house the dog was to come out of was already constructed. In a case of don't raise the bridge, lower the river, I immediately suggested the substitute, a French Bulldog. "A French what?" was the ad agency's question, but they were overjoyed with the solution.

**KEESHOND** Holland, England. Dutch. Politics. Spitz. Wolf Spitz. Northern breed. Huggable.

**LHASA APSO** Upscale, expensive, rich. Yappy. Palace guard. Orient, China, Tibet.

**POODLE (MINIATURE)** Foolish, comical, foppish. Expensive. Yappy. One of the highly recognizable breeds.

**POODLE (STANDARD)** Expensive, upscale. Silly, foppish. Extravagant.

**SCHIPPERKE** Little Captain. Black. Alert, quick, watch dog. Holland, Belgium.

**SHIBA INU** Japan, Orient. Spitz-type. Foxlike. Sharp, aggressive. Self-centered. Independent.

**TIBETAN SPANIEL** Random-bred pet. Cute. Orient, Tibet, China. Beijing. Pekingese mutt. Rough, tough, rugged, macho.

**TIBETAN TERRIER** Tibet, China, Mongolia, Orient. Mid America, generic dog. Pet. Cute, funny, spunky. Alert, watch dog.

## Miscellaneous

The American Kennel Club uses the term "Miscellaneous" for breeds they do not recognize but that *may* be open for later registration.

**AUSTRALIAN KELPIE**   Australia. Dingo. Sheep, sheepherder. Fast, rapid, agile. Random bred.

**BORDER COLLIE**   Generic Collie. Farm Collie. Bright, alert, fast. The ultimate sheepherding breed.

**CANAAN DOG**   Israel. Sharp, quick, rapid, businesslike.

**CAVALIER KING CHARLES SPANIEL**   The nineties. Upscale. Regal, royal. Oil paintings.

**GREATER SWISS MOUNTAIN DOG**   Alpine. Switzerland. Mountains. Massive. Nondescript generic dog.

**NEAPOLITAN MASTIFF**   Macho, huge, aggressive, rugged, immense, tough, Italian Bulldog. Naples. A ferocious guard dog.

**SPINONI ITALIANI**   Nondescript hunting dog.

**TIBETAN MASTIFF**   Massive, huge, giant, gargantuan, strong, machismo. Powerful, aggressive guard dog. Mastiff. Tibet. China. Mongolia. Ultimate guard dog. Successfully used in *Man's Best Friend.*

For those of you in the advertising business, do not use this breed information as your sole guide in selecting your spokesdog or logo for a new product. It is the starting point for you so you can impress your client with your ability to stimulate his business.

Two caveats stated earlier are worth repeating here: (1) Contradictory impressions exist and if not true are still there; and (2) these impressions are age (as well as ethnic and socioeconomic) related.

# ★ CATS

The second most used animal in print, film, theater, television—all areas of the entertainment industry—is the cat. And rightly so. Cats are great. I consider myself a dog person, but cats are easier pets. They are affectionate and require less care than a dog. A neighbor will never complain about the cat barking. Cats are not as close to us as dogs, and because they are independent, do not rely on us as much. Images and impressions of the cat breeds are not as deeply ingrained in our psyche as dog breeds. Cat breeds are not steeped in folklore and urban legend as are dog breeds. Most cat breeds were developed fairly recently, in the twentieth century, and many not until the mid-twentieth century. A short history does not foster traditional imagery.

There are no negative terms if you make every negative a positive. Gaunt or emaciated or Shakespeare's "lean and hungry look" may sound negative, but if you are talking about high fashion, those terms are positive.

Cats, as well as other animals, that have a more child-like appearance wind up being child surrogates to the owners. For this reason the pudgy, flat-faced cats are considered more of a cuddly pet, while the long, lithe, lean cat takes on a high-fashion look. Here are thumbnail sketches of the images evoked by the most popular types and breeds.

**ABYSSINIAN** Lithe, active, athletic, alert, muscular. Ticked. Aloof, regal. Ancient Egypt. Hieroglyphics. Africa. Delicate, airy, wispy.

**AMERICAN CURL** Cuddly, lovable, charming. Mongrel. American. Melting pot.

**AMERICAN SHORTHAIR** Alley cat. American. The ultimate generic cat. While purebred, the breed is the epitome of the mongrel cat. Ratter, mouser. Farm cat.

**AMERICAN WIREHAIR** American. Unique. In photographs the wire coat gives an interesting texture, which the uninitiated will not recognize as a wire coat. This added texture is a decided plus when it is necessary to photograph a black, blue or white cat.

**BALINESE** Lithe, graceful. Wispy, lacy, gauzy, gossamer, diaphanous. Classy, pure. Siam, Bali, Thailand. Expensive. Regal.

**BENGAL** Leopard. Big Cat. Dangerous, deadly, killer.

**BIRMAN** Slothful. Transmogrification. Ethereal, mystical. Sacred cat of Burma. Angora. Tibet, China, India. Reincarnation. Sweet, huggable, cuddly.

**BOMBAY** India. Black cat. Halloween, witches, crones, caldrons. Mysticism. Tarot cards and palm readers. Leopard.

**BRITISH SHORTHAIR** English . . . veddy British. Bright-eyed. Stocky, well put together, massive. Solid power.

**BURMILLA** Burma, England. Sable.

**BURMESE** Burma. If an unusual color is desired in a shoot, look to the Burmese. Stocky.

**CHARTREUX** Chartreuse, green, blue, gray, slate gray. Ethereal, ghostly. France, Brittany.

**COLORPOINT SHORTHAIR** Thin, sleek, elegant. Siam, Thailand.

**CORNISH REX** Silky. Regal. Anorexic, thin, finespun, lean, scraggy, gaunt, meager, wraithlike. King. Majestic.

**CYMRIC** Isle of Man. Angora. Persia. Clown. Fun-loving companion. Playful. Round, chubby, fat, rotund. Heavy, broad, stocky. Kissy-poo, huggable, cuddly.

**DEVON REX** English. Regal, royal, majestic. The Crown. Silky. Lank, spare, slender, thin-bodied, svelte.

**EGYPTIAN MAU** Egypt, Italy, America. Imperial Czar. Hieroglyphics.

**EXOTIC SHORTHAIR**   Baby. Child surrogate. Persian. Cuddly, cute. Bright-eyed and bushy-tailed. Charming, kissy-poo, lovable.

**HAVANA BROWN**   Cubs. Sleek. Exotic. England, Siam. Tobacco, cigars. Gangly, scanty, narrow. What an ad for *Ebony* magazine! A high-fashion model with a Havana Brown advertising Virginia Slims cigarettes.

**JAPANESE BOBTAIL**   Tailless. Delicate, flimsy, frail, light. Japan, China, Korea.

**JAVANESE**   Java. Expensive. Sleek, slinky, exotic.

**KORAT**   Mystical, ethereal, ghostly. Burma, Thailand.

**MAINE COON CAT**   Maine. Raccoon. Early American. Wild. Cute, cuddly, affectionate. Persian. Angora. Alley cat.

**MANX**   Isle of Man. Spanish Rock. Tailless. British.

**NORWEGIAN FOREST CAT**   Sweet, squeezable, lovable. Central Norway. Hunter. Forests, woods, cold streams and brooks. Boxy.

**OCICAT**   Abyssinia, Siam, America. Ocelot.

**ORIENTAL SHORTHAIR**   Thin, meager, sparse. Siam, Bali, Orient.

**ORIENTAL LONGHAIR**   Aesthetic, graceful, slinky, sleek, lithe.

**PERSIAN**   Cute, cuddly, huggable, snuggle, squeeze, embosom, kissy face, adorable, sweet, angelic, caressable. Quiet. Expensive, rich, wealthy. Childlike.

**RAGDOLL**   Nestle, snuggle, embosom. A great cat for the play *I Remember Mama* or any production requiring a placid cat. The large size makes the cat easy to see, and its relaxed attitude makes for a cat that will remain in place. High threshold of pain. Placid. Lounge around.

**RUSSIAN BLUE**  Wraithlike, ethereal, wispy, exotic. Russian.

**SCOTTISH FOLD**  Scotland. Huggable, cute. Unique.

**SCOTTISH FOLD LONGHAIR**  Cute, cuddly, huggable, bundle, nestle, snuggle. Scotland.

**SIAMESE**  Expensive, upscale. Graceful, slinky. Aesthetic, exotic. Slender. Siam. Royal Cat of Siam, regal, king. Delicate, fine-boned. Ancient.

**SINGAPURA**  Lean, lithe, fine. Singapore. Ticked.

**SNOWSHOE**  Winter. Cold.

**SOMALI**  British Ticks. Bunny Cats. Abyssinia, Somalia, Ethiopia.

**SPHYNX**  Egypt, Mexico. Slender, gaunt, "lean and hungry look," slender, reduced, scant, thin skin. Hairless, wafer thin, slip, meager.

**TONKINESE**  Canada. Burma, Siam, Tonkin. Moderate. Mink.

**TURKISH ANGORA**  Turkey, Ankara, Persia. Long-haired white purity. Ancient.

**TURKISH VAN**  Turkey, Armenia. Purity. Ancient. Odd-eyed.

# **IX**

# **The Financial Reward**

> "The reason is
> primarily emo-
> tional: money!"
>
> Robert Downey,
> Jr., in the title
> role of *Chaplin.*

At this point in the book you should realize you are into this for the glamour and romance rather than the money. Don't make me repeat that if money is your only motivation, then get out of the business. There are a lot surer ways of making more money faster than in show Business.

If you are offered one dollar on your first job, take it. You can then say that you have worked in showBiz. Some animal agencies get nervous when the owner just seems to be interested in money. You, like everyone else, are entitled to be paid for your services. To get along, you have to know when to go along with what you are offered. When and *if* your animal becomes a big-time, big-name star, then you can negotiate. Remember, the human actors who become "overnight successes" have been working at their craft for twenty years before that success. If you are working for an animal agency, they will tell you what they will pay. *Take it!* That first job is all important.

If you are not working through an animal agency, a good rule of thumb is to check and see what a human actor with lines is paid. I charge more for an animal that has to do with something specific. Figure what it is worth to you to do the job and then double the figure. You can always come down, but you cannot go up in price. If they want to bargain on your price, explain that instead of a single actor they are getting you and your pet: two for the price of one. You also have special transportation requirements for the animal. Buy some type of carrier. Not only does it establish that you do have "special transportation requirements," but it also will make your job easier on the set. Your Tasmanian wild dog can curl up in a crate and not be pestered by curious crew members.

"What's your quote?" is a term in the business; it means, What did you make on your last job? This doesn't mean that serious negotiations have started—it is hard to check out your quote—but it is a starting point. If you come up with a price and they halve it, turn them down. Counter-offer with a higher price and some intangible, such as being transported back and forth by limousine. They'll balk at this, but if they have a limo ordered and it is not for the exclusive use of some superstar, they may go along. Limos are not normally given to animal actors, but if you get that limo one time, you can always add to your quote, "And I usually get a limo." You may not get the limo, but you will impress them. In stage work you should insist on a private dressing room. In film work, during negotiating time, you can insist on a credit. You should get it anyhow, and if they get sticky on the price, start to specify type size and location of the credit. It will slow down their poor-mouth pleadings, but they won't give that to you unless you have the next Rin-Tin-Tin. When you do have the next Rin-Tin-Tin, hire a hard-hitting agent who will get you all kinds of big money. Another stopper is to ask for final cut on the animal work. That's final selection and approval of the final film footage. That they will never give you.

If you are used for atmosphere or background work without the animal doing something specific, then the job is worth a good deal less money. There are a number of different pay scales for "extras," and you should at least get that kind of money if you are working directly for the production company, but I would strive to get "silent bit," paying a bit more. The more frugal production companies that need a dog for atmosphere will hire an actor with a pooch at the current union rate of about $20 extra. It won't even cover cab fare, but actors are a hungry lot and so eager to work that they sell themselves and their pet cheaply. Current rates can be obtained from the Screen Actors Guild (see Appendix 1 for address).

Animal actors do not receive residuals (see Appendix 3, the Glossary). The fact that you do not get residuals is a good "argument" when negotiating price. While it is a good argument, it will not make any difference to the production company because they are not involved in the paying of residuals. If you work with an animal agency, you will not be involved in the negotiations. They will tell you what you will be paid. You may be working on a nonunion job in which no one is getting residuals. Even in a nonunion job you are entitled to a decent wage. *Some* nonunion jobs pay people even more money than union jobs because they are not paying the union pension and welfare. Even if you are pro-union, do not let that outlook affect taking a job. Take every job that comes down the pike. There is no union for animal actors.

Getting jobs directly is extremely difficult. There are a number of theatrical publications that can help you find out about up-and-coming projects. Some of them contain casting notices that will keep you abreast of what is developing, but as a rule they do not list animal casting. While subscribing to one or all of these periodicals will develop your knowledge of the business, it doesn't pay to subscribe if you *only* use them to find out about casting. The oldest and original New York weekly newspaper supplying casting notices is Leo Schull's *Show Business,* which lists nonunion and student films as well as union jobs. Another

New York weekly, *Back Stage,* was founded by a former employee of Schull. It is a slicker publication but contains less casting information. It now has a West Coast edition. The venerable *Variety,* the oldest in the field, has a weekly (New York) and a daily (Los Angeles) edition. The daily *Hollywood Reporter* is published on the "left" coast.

# ★ THE JOBS, AND WHAT THEY'RE WORTH

A thousand words into this chapter and I haven't mentioned actual money yet. Now to some prices! They are current as of this writing and can be higher. We all know that prices keep going up, but not in the animal rental field. Just realize that if you have a rare, exotic or unique animal, such as an Anegada ground iguana, it is worth more than the quoted prices.

## Animal Act Assistant

As an assistant to an animal act, you are really being taken on as an apprentice and should be prepared to work for somewhere between minimum wage and $250 per week. Be prepared to do menial work, with the emphasis on moving feces from point A to point B. You have to pay your dues.

They tell the story about the circus hand who complained about cleaning up the enormous amount of elephant droppings. When it was suggested that if he was unhappy he should quit, his answer was, "What, and get out of show business?"

## Animal Acts

If you have developed an animal act, be prepared to work for nothing while you break it in. The local children's hospital, Rotary and Lions clubs, etc. would love to have you for nothing. An act running twenty to forty minutes, playing to small groups, should make at least $75 to $150 per show. Animal acts are naturals for children's parties, but there is a reluctance to book them for adult groups. You need a hook to get working with adults. Bear in mind that people who book this type of entertainment do not work on a straight 10 percent commission. They will add $50 to $150 to the price. Now if you get a week in Las Vegas opening for Frank Sinatra, look for $2,500 a week, but you better be top drawer to open for Ol' Blue Eyes. The actual range in Vegas would be between $1,500 and $5,000 per week, depending on the prestige of your act and for whom you are opening. Francis Albert probably wouldn't let an animal act open for him, not even Siegfried and Roy.

## Commercials

For commercials, an animal agency/animal renter would charge a minimum of $450 for an eight-hour day. You would be paid between $50 and $250 for the day. If you think that is an unfair split, then go into the animal agency business yourself. Be prepared to locate elusive and high-priced liability insurance, rent office space, get a USDA license, install phones, be prepared to man those phones, hire an answering service, put together an advertising budget and deal with a host of other things. Charge time and a half for the ninth and tenth hour and double time after that. You can and should charge for excessive travel time and mileage for your vehicle. Thirty cents a mile is a logical price unless you are transporting two dolphins in a custom-made rig with a full pool on the back.

Even if the animal is already trained to do something specific, charge extra. You gave your pet that extra training and should be paid for it. Two examples: dogs that scratch themselves on cue or will grab a postman's pants leg. The first trick generates about one call every four years and the second a call every year and a half. Generally they want a dog that doesn't look like any of the dogs that you have trained to do this exercise. The production company has a dozen ideas how to "fake" these two tricks, even in a still shot. Believe me, they cannot be faked! The dog has to do them. Meat in the trouser leg will not do it. A dog that retrieves will not look as if he is actually pulling on the trousers. Still shot or film, the dog must actually pull to make it look real.

I was hired one time with a dog that was not trained to scratch. They didn't want to pay the preproduction costs to have the dog trained and intended to use itching powder on the dog. I told them it wouldn't work. It didn't. It was a still shot, and I suggested using some string to position the dog's hindquarters. No, that wouldn't work, they would have the expense of airbrushing the string out. Let me try. No! We never got the shot. They called me back. This time they had the solution. The veterinarian would give the dog an innoculation and that would cause the dog to scratch. I explained that the dog would scratch once or twice and they probably wouldn't get the shot. I didn't even want to do the job a second time, but I had a moral obligation. On the appointed day the dog was given the innoculation, scratched twice, and they didn't get the shot. They had egg on their face. I was charging them a two-hour minimum and we had nothing to do. I again suggested the string and they said no. Well, we were all at the studio with nothing to do and they finally relented. The string worked and it was a very successful ad campaign.

Sometimes you will be asked to quote a half-day rate. Charge 70 to 80 percent of your full day rate with overtime starting after four hours. Make sure that you get a reporting time at least twenty-four hours in advance. Don't stand by waiting for them to call you in on the day of the commercial. This way you can properly schedule your day. If they go into overtime that is their problem, not yours. Going into overtime will seldom happen because they already have figured out the shooting schedule to the minute. I hate giving half-day rates and often will refuse to quote them.

## Films and TV

The money for films and television is about the same as for commercials. I like to quote about the same amount of money a scale actor would receive on a low-budget film. Scale for a film is about $431 per day at this writing. I charge a minimum of $450 per day, which is higher than this rule of thumb, but I think an animal is worth it. In California they will quote $250 for the animal and $200 for the handler. If you have to train an animal to do something specific for a film or TV, you can charge for that specific training. Refer to it as preproduction costs. That they understand! Filming is not as exciting as you might imagine. You spend a lot of time hanging around. Be prepared to hurry up and wait and bring a couple of good books along. Make one of them *How to Get Your Pet Into Show Business.*

## Stage

Remember the Captain Haggerty Show Business Law of Inverse Proportions on Remuneration. The more work involved, the less money paid. This law applies to human actors as well as to animal actors. A stage play requires more work and time than a film. In a play you have to be there thirty to forty hours per week, and sometimes more. You are under tremendous stress. The animal *cannot* make

Burt Reynolds, on camera with the author. ShowBiz is not all fun and games. This scene from *Shamus* illustrates one of the many doors that are opened for you when supplying animals.

Dolly Parton, in a horse-drawn carriage supplied by Chateau Theatrical Animals of New York City. Chateau specializes in horses and the right equipment, although they do supply other animals. The famous carriage rides through Central Park are usually done by Chateau's animals. Photo: Gloria McGill, Chateau Theatrical Animals.

Frank Inn, the Big Daddy of showbiz animal handlers, with Benji, the dog that became more famous than the actors he starred with. Frank not only worked with dogs but also with many other animals. Another of Frank's protégés, Arnold the Pig, from the TV series "Green Acres," is in Hollywood's wax museum.

Raquel Welch, with the author, on location in Boston shooting the film *Fuzz*.
Photo: Wally Page.

Morris the Cat, the most famous cat in the business. Morris, handled by trainer Bob Martwick, is the "spokescat" for 9-Lives cat food.

Petey became popular beyond belief when the *Our Gang* comedies were shown on television. When Pit Bull Terriers receive unfavorable press, Petey is always mentioned as an excellent example of the breed.

Rin-Tin-Tin, the grand-daddy of theatrical dogs and the model of a well-trained movie dog, became the best-known German Shepherd in the world.

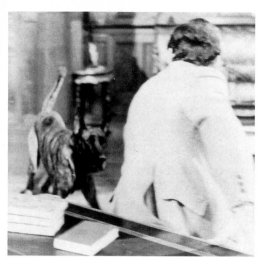

This sequence of pictures shows Burt Reynolds being attacked by the Great Dane Jai. Jai was handled and trained by Bob Maida. Photos: Bob Maida, Manassas, Virginia.

Jai grabs Burt Reynolds' arm in *Shamus*. Burt does all his own stunt work.

No, not again! Burt Reynolds on the floor, well-known character actor Ron Weyand in the background and Captain Haggerty holding Jai await further instructions from director Buzz Kulik on reshooting the attack scene.

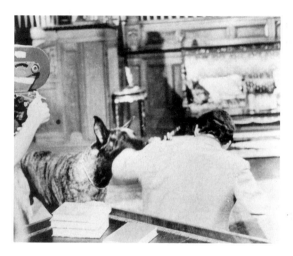

Ralph Helfer developed a career with wild animals that was unmatched by anyone, including Frank Buck. Here Ralph, who lives half the year with the animals of Africa, rides a white rhino.

Chumley the Bulldog was an oft-mentioned dog in Flip Wilson's comedy routine. When it came time for Chumley to be seen, Mike Jones had the job of producing the dog. When Flip Wilson was on "The Tonight Show," it was necessary to produce a whole row of Bulldog fans that were introduced from the audience. Mike Jones also handled this job. Photo: Wally Page.

Irwin Keyes, well-known character actor, on location with Macho Martinez (*left*) and Cha-Chi Martinez (*right*). Irwin is holding a face mask from "Frankenstein General Hospital," in which he played the title role.

Bob Weatherwax and the legendary Lassie. Bob is the second generation of three generations of studio dog trainers. Bob's father was the late, great Rudd Weatherwax, and Bob's son, Bob Jr., is successfully carrying on in the family tradition.

Dan Haggerty, with one of the bears that made him famous in the role of Grizzly Adams. Photo: Roger Montgomery

Tim Welch in a clown costume with Bailey, one of his dogs from Welch's Sheltie Circus.

Thumbalina, Teddy Bear, and Bailey—all from Welch's Sheltie Circus doing their act on stage. Their owner, Brian Timothy Welch, had the desire and vision to move his dogs forward into a successful career, even though he lived in a remote area of Pennsylvania, far from the center of show business.

The author with a Boston Terrier in a studio shooting a TV commercial.

Mug-Z, a multitalented dog, has done well over 150 TV commercials. Her owner/trainer is Kathy Mills Ahearn.

Cowboy Joe Phillips has made a lifelong career out of his love of horses. Here he is riding Goldie.

The author and a tiny Chihuahua on location in Mexico, shooting a film.

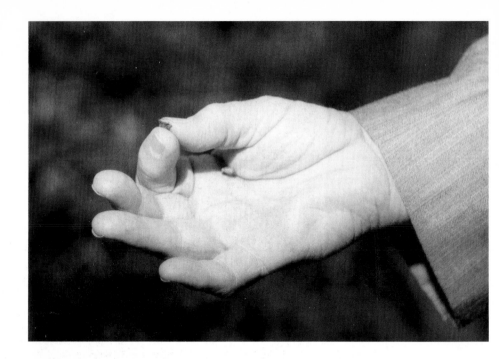

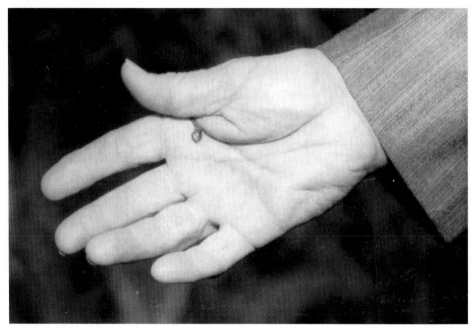

How to handle food when using it as a reward. The food is fed to the animal from the thumb and forefinger, with another piece ready to replace it by holding it in the anatomical snuff box. Photos: Jeff Haymes.

A piece of food being held in the anatomical snuff box.

a mistake. For that week's work you make about twice as much as you will on a single day shooting a film. Stage work is the hardest type of work, and very time consuming.

Broadway is the top of the heap and pays $950 per week for human actors. If the animal is atmosphere, forget about it. It is more trouble than it's worth, unless you are supplying a number of animals that don't require one handler per animal. If the play is a bomb, it certainly doesn't pay. No one can really tell if it will be a hit. A critic may have gotten up on the wrong side of the bed the morning of opening night. To make money, you need a long run. Demand a run-of-the-play contract. Start-up costs are high.

## Fashion Shows

Fashion shows can be lucrative. They are a good starting point in that, generally, the animal does not need a lot of training. If some fashion designer comes up with a "bird of prey" fashion theme for American-made clothes, what would be more appropriate than your bald eagle perched on a model's forearm? Make sure that the model is properly garbed with a protective glove, and Ben, your eagle, should have on his jesses and, more importantly, his rufter. Coping (trimming) to the bill and talons should be done shortly before the fashion show. Are you going to find a model strong enough to support Ben? I doubt it. On something simple I would say $125 per hour with a two-hour minimum. They normally pay by the job rather than by the hour, but that doesn't preclude you from quoting an hourly rate. Remember, if you have something exotic and specific and needed like Ben, you should get more. Ben doesn't work for chicken feed. He can eat a lot of mice between jobs.

## Promotions

Promotions are different and for this reason a little more interesting. Usually the animal is there for a look, for appearance, rather than to do anything. Occasionally, however, they'll want the animal to do something, like the time a call came asking me for a kangaroo. Not an impossible job, but the client wanted the kangaroo to hand out flowers to people. She was to carry these bouquets in her pouch!

The right promotions can be repeated a number of times in different sections of the country, which means travel if you have an exotic animal or one trained to do what is needed. Get the same rates as a model will get. In promotions they will probably be looking for a beautiful woman to work with the animal, and if the model has to talk or deliver a prepared speech, a more expensive model will be hired; this increases the budget and also the money you receive. There is a wide price range for these jobs, and while an animal agency might try to get $100 per hour and pay you $25 to $50 per hour, the customer will try to negotiate a flat price for a job running two to five hours at $250 to $350, with you netting $100 to $200.

## Print Jobs

In a print job photographs are taken to illustrate an ad. In an indoor shoot there are few problems. Outdoors, make sure that the models do not drop the leash if they are handling a dog. Explain to them the importance of holding and controlling the animal. If you get a couple of attractive print ads under your belt, they will help you start a portfolio.

Generally a print job is easy work that pays $85 to $150 per hour. Always try to get a two-hour minimum. An animal agency will pay you $25 to $50 an hour but *may* absorb some expenses such as gas, tolls, and parking.

Point of purchase and packaging can be very lucrative if handled properly—clients are used to paying extra for this type of work. Your animal's photo will appear in a retail store at a big display advertising the product. This is point of purchase. The added exposure should be worth more money. If your pet's photo will appear on every package, you can make a great deal of money getting a fraction of a penny on each unit sold. Just imagine! A top-flight actor or model can demand a high fee, but it is more difficult with an animal. Remember, if they love your animal and will use no other, you have a better chance. A bonus of $850 for a human model to appear on a package on a "buy out" is a low figure that is paid. This is in addition to the shooting fee. If you can get it, fine. Know what your bargaining position is before getting too hard-nosed. This is an area where it will really pay to use a hard-charging agent.

## ★ EXCLUSIVITY

Should your animal sign up exclusively with an animal agency/animal renter, assuming there is one in your area? That is a many-sided question, and you have to be aware of how the business works. To begin with, human actors do not necessarily sign up exclusively with one theatrical agent. In LA most actors are "signed," and in NYC most actors freelance. A human actor without an agent in LA will get no work, but in New York this is not true. The Robert Redfords and the Meryl Streeps are signed because they cannot be bothered with such mundane matters as money. And money is how success is measured in show Business. An agent is better able than you to negotiate price. Remember that people supplying animals in this crazy business are not really agents. They are animal packagers.

If you have a Benji, it is best to sign an exclusive contract. If you have a "potential" Benji, the answer may be a little different. You want to get your Benji all the work you can. It is too early in the animal's career to pick and choose. Canvass all the animal theatrical agents in your area and hound them. Knock on their doors. They will submit you.

Exclusivity is a two-way street. You can't work for anyone else, but the agent has got to bust his or her chops to get you work. I remember submitting a Bulldog one time. The owner of this Bulldog was freelancing with every agent in town. Not necessarily a bad idea, but this time it was. One of the people receiving the submission said, "Not this one again. Does everyone have this dog?" I said, "Yes, I use the Bulldog too. It's a great dog. The reason I submitted this one is because I thought you were worried about price. I'd recommend this other Bulldog, but he's a little more expensive and worth it." Sure it was a better dog. It cost more. That made it better. I was also the only agent who had this dog listed. I booked the job!

I remember training a dog for a very successful Broadway show. The owner and handler of the animal, in a circuitous way, asked me to represent him. I felt this was a conflict of interest. While I was working with and training this animal handler, I was being paid by the production company that was putting on the play. I didn't think that he needed an agent. He would have been better off getting a regular theatrical agent to handle the negotiations. He foolishly signed an exclusive with an animal agency, and while they got him more money, the honeymoon was very short, and they didn't get along too well. The next thing I knew the other animal agency was doing the road shows of the play, not their "exclusive" client. It was apparent where their interests lay. To my mind, they were not ethical, while I was ethical to the extreme. I could have made a lot more money being unethical, but if I was unethical, I wouldn't have this little story to tell. Be ethical. Be honest. Be fair. It doesn't cost; it pays in peace of mind.

If someone wants to sign you to an exclusive because they want to submit your cat as the spokescat for XYZ cat food, I would take pen to the dotted line. I might ask for some type of financial guarantee, which is a realistic request. If the agency says that they haven't gotten to the money stage, that is believable and I'd still sign, with the proviso that all bets are off if they don't land the account. Don't worry about the money. It will be there if they select your pet as the spokescat. You see, once they make a decision, they are locked into it. Getting them to make the decision is the tough job. Once it's made, it's etched in stone. Too many people have approved the spokescat, and it would cause internecine problems within the agency and between the agency and the client.

You can make a buck supplying animals, but if you come up with a Lassie or a Morris, you have a lifetime career. You can't win it unless you're in it. And I hope you make more money than there are spots in the *101 Dalmatians*.

# X

# Networking and Negotiating

"The friends you make from business are better than the business you make from friends."

Haggerty's Postulate on Business Relationships

You can build your business on networking. Ask people for favors. Your school chum is now a successful screenwriter. Contact him. Butter him up. Ask for an introduction. You are not using your friend. You are networking. You are using one another. How does this differ from Haggerty's Postulate on Business Relationships? You do not want to do business with your high school buddy. He'll want a deal. He'll want a kickback. He'll want something you don't want to give or do. Doing business with him will be aggravation. You probably weren't that good friends back in old Nostalgia High. On the other hand, his contacts will work out well for you. You'll do a good job for them and they'll tell Ted Screenwriter what a pro you are. It is a feather in Ted's cap that he has such great contacts. You'll become fast friends with Ted's friend. Greater friends than you were with old Ted because the friendship flows from the business, not the other way around.

# ★ NETWORKING THE SMART WAY

Most people do not know how to network. They approach it with the wrong attitude. "What can you do for me?" is wrong. It should be "What can I do for you?" Look to the Godfather. The successful Godfather did things for others. Always put out more than you expect back. Since 1983, I have been having showBiz people sign my "I Owe You One" card. The card says, "Everyone tells you 'I owe you one' in this business. Not only do I owe you one because"—and here is a blank that I fill in. The card continues, "but I'm signing this marker as proof. I will even return your phone calls." I only had two people refuse to sign it. A line producer, who I never did trust, and a professional con man. Perhaps there is no difference between a professional con man and a producer. Everyone else gleefully signed, and I've built up quite a collection. It is one way to remind them that they were supposed to help you out. That they were supposed to make it up on the next job. It keeps them honest.

# ★ NEGOTIATING

You are in trouble when you get your first job. You don't know how to negotiate the price. There is no one to handle the negotiating for you. If you are working through an animal agent, take what you are offered. After all it is your first job!

Know the difference between when you are being called to help the production company quote a job and when they are really serious. If the production company is making up a price on a job they, naturally, have to know the cost factors. They don't have the job yet. The price they quote will have a bearing on their getting the job. In any event you usually cannot give them a firm price because the person they have making phone calls and getting quotes lacks knowledge and authority. That person cannot give the information you need to give them a bottom-line cost. That's why I like the California approach to quoting prices. How much is the animal? "$250." That's just the animal. The handler will cost you another $200 for the day. How does this differ from the New York method? They'll tell you $450. That is for animal and handler. If they are just calling for quotes, that means that they are bidding on the job. Now is the time to follow up. Establish a relationship. The person who called you has no authority and won't be there when it is time to do the job. Get a name. Find out the name of the person with whom you should follow up.

A good rule of thumb in negotiating is to have someone do the negotiating for you. An agent. Agents don't cost, they pay. Ten percent of nothing is nothing, but 10 percent of a million dollars I'll gladly give up. You'll never get the million dollars by yourself.

I remember, many years ago, doing a job through someone who was acting as an agent/expeditor. She pulled together all the pieces the production company couldn't or wouldn't handle. It was a TV commercial for a product that was a great idea, except it didn't work. I had better not mention the name. I hope that all of those involved moved on to bigger and better things. The product certainly didn't. It was a toy that permitted children to interact with it and a ball. The commercial was to show this, and they wanted a dog to play with the ball. I have to be careful here not to be too specific, to protect the innocent as well as the guilty. A dog was chosen, and we thought the job would be a piece of cake. Mike Jones, a very fine trainer, was given the job of putting it together. Problem number one was that the ball was several millimeters too big for the dog's mouth. The other problem was that the ball had a metal coating, and dogs have a reputation for not retrieving metal. We had a month to work on it. No, we didn't get another dog. When a specific dog is locked in, you have no choice. You can't go changing animals once the "creatives" have made their decision, no matter how imprudent it may be. And we didn't put the dog on a "jaw stretcher," either. We found balls that were just a little bit bigger, and the dog willingly stretched his jaw to catch them. It is the old story about touching your toes. If you can't do it today, just keep stretching, and in a week or so you will be able to do the job. The metal problem we overcame because it was such fun for the dog to chase and catch the ball. The problem we couldn't control was the fact that the damned toy kept breaking down. In typical Madison Avenue fashion, the backup toys rapidly appeared on the scene. We shot the commercial, and it was dynamite. The product was rotten, but the commercial was great. An advertising axiom says that "Nothing will destroy a poor product faster than good advertising." I haven't heard of the product since the commercial started to be shown. We had a lot of aggravation on the job, and we were entitled to be paid the money we received. The money we received was about twice what we would have foolishly quoted on the job. Remember, agents pay.

## ★ FINDING AN AGENT

Now is the time for you to get an agent . . . if you feel you need one. The real animal work is in locating an agent. You are entering the territory of sharks and wolves. Real agents will negotiate anything. Are they qualified to negotiate your work? Probably not, but they are really qualified to negotiate. Choose an agent who has experience in negotiating for people in a wide range of activities in the business: actors, directors, writers, etc. Believe me, a good agent will ask for, and get, things you didn't even know existed. The best ones don't have time to handle you, but you do have a unique situation, and that may pique the interest of the better agents. The better agent may do it for a lark. He or she won't stay around too long because you won't bring in enough money. Save that agent for the more interesting and potentially more lucrative jobs. They like to brag to their fellow agents, "Your star client, hah! I got more for a cat than she got on her last film! And I got the cat better billing!" There are also managers and even lawyers who, more properly, should be handling you. You can have more protection dealing with an agent than with a manager. Agents are generally licensed by the state and/or unions and take 10 percent. This percentage is often controlled by union regulations or state law. Managers generally take 15 to 25 percent and up, depending on how much managing they are doing. Lawyers are also licensed and *should* be further controlled by the state bar association, but you know what they say about lawyers. Your deals normally will not be complex enough to require a lawyer. Whoever you choose must have experience in the theatrical field. If not, you will be throwing away the 10, 15 or 25 percent you are paying them. There are even those referred to as "100 percenters" in the business: the animal handlers/trainers. Not true, but cute!

Personal recommendation, networking, is the best way to locate the right person to handle your negotiating. The good ones will not even talk to you unless they have a personal recommendation from a *shtarker*. The agent will not know your business, so it is up to you to educate her or him. A gift of a copy of this book is a great way to start.

Be prepared to handle negotiating yourself. Things happen fast in this business, and you will have to know something about what is happening.

When completely out of your element upon being asked a price, try "What do you have in the budget?" This is a legitimate and fair question that is often asked. The question may be thrown back at you, but once you have taken this tack stay with it. Remember, the first one who answers loses. Your silence will cause them to make you an offer. Even if the money is beyond your wildest dreams, don't jump at it. Be kind to your opposite. Do not let her know that she has offered you too much. Your hemming and hawing will convince her that she offered you too little and make her feel good. You are not looking for a situation where you win and your opponent loses. You want a "win-win" situation where all parties are happy. You are not trying to win. You are trying to get as much money as possible. I prefer to have set prices. That way I do not have to bargain. Take it or leave it. Some people love to bargain, and if you know you are up against someone like this, double your price and let him hock you down 20 percent or even 30 percent. Both of you will be very happy.

# ★ POSITIONAL VS. WIN-WIN NEGOTIATING

Positional negotiating is, from both parties' points of view, the least desirable. Positional negotiating is "This is what I want and this is what I'll pay. Period."

The problem with positional negotiating is

1. It conceals each party's true needs.

2. It is stressful as an adversarial or combative situation.

3. It, surprisingly enough, takes more time.

This hard-nosed approach is only good on a short-term basis. You will never develop a good relationship. In positional negotiating each party is trying to take advantage of the other. This makes for poor agreements. I was renting a dog at one time and the person requesting the services had a question about the contract. I explained that the contract said he would forfeit his deposit if he didn't pay his bill. "I'm not going to sign that!" he replied. We hadn't even signed the contract and he was planning to renege on paying the bill! That was fine with me. There would be no contract. A poor negotiating technique but a good business decision. There are people with whom you do not want to do business.

Win-win negotiating is the way to go! I never want to do business with someone who can't make money or come out ahead from my work. If they can't make money, how will they be able to pay me? From a negotiating point of view, that is not the best approach. It does, however, take into consideration what you consider a day's pay. It's important in quoting prices. There is no sense losing money doing a job. Paul Goldie, mentioned earlier in this book, can make six times more per hour in his full-time job as a computer programmer, but he has a passion for working with theatrical animals. He makes less money doing what he enjoys. After all, what enjoyment can you get out of petting a computer?

When I was working in New York, a production agency wanted a quote for a product that was being introduced, Alamo dog food. For four months they had been working with a trainer who was supposed to put the job together. Three dogs of different sizes, when asked by the lady of the house, were to answer, à la barber shop quartet, "AL—A—MO." Each dog would deliver one syllable of the name with a singer's voice dubbed in over the barking. On the surface it seemed to be a simple job of getting the dogs to bark on cue, but I knew it was more difficult than that. Not only did they have to bark on cue, they also had to bark in the right sequence *and* in the right tempo. It was a tough job, and I offered to supply the one dog that the other trainer said he was unable to supply because it was "sick." I figured they had been working on this job four months and I, by supplying one dog, would get one-third of the blame if anything went wrong. They were shooting in less than a week, and they said they would get back in touch with me. Maybe the other trainer really didn't have the other two dogs ready, either. Anyway, the production company was completely turned off by the trainer, who had put them out on a limb. They were committed. They had client approval. They wanted me to handle the entire job. That meant added expenses. It was my kind of job. It was a challenge, and no one else seemed able to do it. I knew I didn't have to spend four months of my life prepping the job. It would take work and preparation, but less than a week. And of course, money was no object. They didn't even discuss money. They wanted the job done. That is a great approach in negotiating with me. If I don't discuss money, it clears my mind of even thinking about it. It also showed they had a great deal of confidence in me. In this type of situation I never burn them with a high price. I was in luck with two fine handler/trainers who had the dogs of varying sizes. Jimmy Soto had a Saint Bernard and an American Staffordshire Terrier and Ilsa Walzer had a fine apricot Miniature Poodle. We did the job with no problems. The production company was overjoyed. They became fans and gave me a lot of business over the years.

There are a number of considerations in my type of negotiation. Never negotiate with a stranger; first, establish a relationship. And keep your promise. Remember, your word is your bond. My agent claims that ad agencies and production companies keep throwing new people at the agents. The reason is that they do not want their people establishing a relationship with the various commercial and theatrical agencies because it will *give* the agents too much of a bargaining tool. *Clarification:* Do not confuse advertising agencies with commercial and theatrical agents. Advertising agencies work for the client and agents work for the talent (animal or human).

Haggerty's Axiom on Business Agreements is "A contract is only as good as the people making it." This applies to written contracts, too. To quote Samuel Goldwyn, "A verbal contract isn't worth the paper it's written on."

Including preproduction costs in all bids is a wise move. Production people are used to preproduction costs. If you have to give the animal special training in preparation to do the job, you should be reimbursed for your time. When you promise them you will get the required training in on the animal and are unsuccessful, it is unethical to charge for that preproduction training. When the time is short and you say you will try your best, then you can charge. It is not your fault if they never give you enough time. It is really nobody's fault—it is the nature of the business. There is never enough time in the initial shooting, but there is all the time in the world on the reshoot. If the specialized training is already in the animal you should explain that and say that you are charging more for the job because this particular animal is highly trained.

Remember, intangibles are important negotiating tools. A limo or better hotel accommodations than the rest of the cast and crew is another intangible that has a basis. An agent can't get 10 percent of an intangible, but they'll try to get it for you as a courtesy. You can't have an animal with the rest of the group. They won't like it. After all your pet is a *star!* Think of the publicity value of the animal living in the Presidential Suite while the star has a room overlooking the alley. Work for those intangibles such as the limo, hotel and flying the Concorde. If they spend more money on you, they are convincing themselves how important you are. These expenses come out of another section of the budget and will go unnoticed. Your pet's prestige will not go unnoticed.

I was supplying two dogs for the production of *Giselle* put on by the visiting Berne (Switzerland) Ballet at the Brooklyn Academy of Music in New York. The perfect dogs belonged to a prominent TV soap opera star. The money she received for the dogs was unimportant to her. Her dogs were with the Berne Ballet. Her friends in the business wanted to know what the dogs were getting paid. They had to know the dogs' quote. I did some fast figuring on the short period of time the dogs were on stage and came up with a per-minute rate that, when extrapolated and compared to this *extremely* well paid soap star's rate, showed the dogs were making more than she did. I told her to tell her friends that the dogs were being paid more than she received. She glowed. That was an answer her friends could gleefully accept. They knew that the money was not as important as the status it conveyed. I never knew what she was making, but by figuring a per-minute, on-stage rate and multiplying it by 60 minutes to the hour and 40 hours in a week, we could honestly say the dogs were making more than she did per week. Her friends couldn't very well ask the star what she was making, but they knew it was a lot. And her dogs made even more money!

The one intangible they will *never* give you is final cut. Tell them you want final cut on the animal work and the bargaining will stop.

## ★ TEN GOLDEN RULES OF NEGOTIATING

**1.** Everything is negotiable.

**2.** No price is final.

**3.** Keep your options open.

4. Have someone handle your negotiating so that you are always the good guy—and can rescue the deal if necessary. Never, never make your agent look bad. An agent has to work with these people more often than you and will have to deal with them again. This is not a "good guy, bad guy" approach but rather a "good guy, better guy" ploy.

5. Try to work with people you know.

6. Look for a win-win situation.

7. Make sure that the people you are negotiating with can make money—or look good if they aren't paying the bills out of their pocket.

8. Always negotiate with the decision makers. If you get into negotiating, it probably will be with a decision maker.

9. If it is a back-and-forth negotiation (What does the budget call for? How much ya want?) keep your mouth shut! The first one that speaks loses.

10. The previously mentioned intangibles are important and give you a good fall-back position.

# Appendixes

# APPENDIX 1

# Useful Addresses

## ★ UNIONS

You can contact unions for all kinds of information. The best information for your purposes is what human actors are paid. Your animal, playing a principal role, is entitled to the same money. There are other unions, but these are the ones that you might need.

**ACTOR'S EQUITY ASSOCIATION**   Represents stage actors and some cabaret and other types of live performance. *165 West 46th St., New York, NY 10036.*

**AMERICAN FEDERATION OF TELEVISION AND RADIO ARTISTS** Handles radio and TV. AFTRA's TV rates and contract are the same as those of the Screen Actors Guild. Both unions have been discussing a merger for years. Believe me, your pet will *not* get any radio work. *260 Madison Ave., New York, NY 10016.*

**AMERICAN GUILD OF VARIETY ARTISTS**   Covers those performers who are working on stage in a variety act. This is the union for those with an animal act. *164 Fifth Ave., New York, NY 10019.*

**SCREEN ACTORS GUILD**   Represents actors in film and some filmed TV shows. There is overlapping in authority between AFTRA and SAG. *5757 Wilshire Blvd., Los Angeles, CA 90036.*

**INTERNATIONAL BROTHERHOOD OF TEAMSTERS**   A very strong and powerful union. Do not mess with the Teamsters. Rent the film *Hoffa.* You may need to join this union if you do a lot of studio work. *25 Louisiana Ave., N.W., Washington, DC 2001.*

# ★ GROUPS AND ORGANIZATIONS

The addresses of organizations mentioned in the book are given below. You may want to contact them to advance your pet's professional career.

**AMERICAN KENNEL CLUB**  A purebred dog registry that holds tremendous power over its member clubs. The AKC wants their clubs to perform community service. You may want to ride on their coattails, while helping the local club, by performing training demonstrations at hospitals and other locations. Your pet would ideally be an AKC registerable purebred. The AKC also confers training degrees. Contact them for regulations. *51 Madison Ave., New York, NY 10010.*

**DELTA SOCIETY**  An organization that is interested in the human-animal bond. They register therapy dogs. *321 Burnett Ave. South, 3rd floor, Renton, WA 98055-2569.*

**THERAPY DOGS INTERNATIONAL**  If your dog does therapy work under their banner, you can be covered by insurance. They, like the Delta Society, register therapy dogs. They do get work. *Therapy Dogs International, Elaine Smith, Secretary, 1536 Morris Pl., Hillsdale, NJ 07205.*

**UNITED STATES DEPARTMENT OF AGRICULTURE**  This organization exercises control over various groups and individuals that supply animals for exhibition to the general public. *Theoretically* you should be licensed by the USDA any time that you exhibit your animal. If you do your work through a USDA-licensed animal organization, you will be covered. Licensing is conducted through the local offices.

Again, *technically*, if you are involved with a local theater group that is putting on *Annie* or *The Wiz*, you should be licensed. Licensing is simple, easy and relatively inexpensive, or should be unless you deal with someone who thinks you are Ringling Brothers and Barnum and Bailey Circus. There is a provision for a no-cost "registration" for those involved in the above-described theater group. Do not provoke the ire of Big Brother in Washington by flaunting your disobedience of his rules. The main office will give you the appropriate regional office to contact. *Staff Director, USDA/APHIS/REAC Rm. 565, Federal Building, 6505 Belcrest Rd., Hyattsville, MD 20782. 301 436-7833.*

**UNITED KENNEL CLUB** A purebred dog organization that conducts obedience trials and confers training degrees. They also publish a number of interesting dog magazines. *100 East Kilgore Rd., Kalamazoo, MI 49001.*

# ★ FILM COMMISSIONERS

The job of film commissioners is to make things easy for film makers to operate in their locations. The organizations listed here are members of the Association of Film Commissioners International. This list is a valuable resource. Use it!

They have to know all the answers. One of the questions is: "Where can I get trained animals locally?" You are part of the answer. Make sure they know about you. You are dealing with bureaucrats, so do not expect creativity. You will have to supply that.

I went to the Palm Beach area to do research for this book. Prior to my arrival I asked someone to locate the names of some animal agencies that I could interview, and he was unsuccessful. This book, on computer disc, was with me. Because I wanted to add to the film commissioners' list, I went to the Palm Beach County Film Liaison Office. When I asked for the names of people who supplied animals I was told, "I never had anyone ask that question before!" While this could indicate there is very little business in Florida, I knew better. There is a tremendous amount of film work done in Florida. This indicated to me that the animal agencies were not doing *their* job of keeping the film commissioners informed. The film office was doing its job, however, and with some fast research gave me the phone numbers of eight firms in southern Florida that supplied all sorts of animals from fish to Kodiak bears.

# ★ THE UNITED STATES AND TERRITORIES

USDA-Forest Service,
Public Affairs
201 14th Street S.W.
Washington, DC 20250

202 205-1438
Fax: 202 205-0885

## ALABAMA
Alabama Film Office
401 Adams Avenue
Montgomery, AL 36130

800 633-5898, 205 242-4195
Fax: 205 242-4086

## ALASKA
Alaska Film Office
3601 "C" Street, Suite 700
Anchorage, AK 99503

907 562-4163
FAX: 907 563-3575

# ARIZONA

Navajo Broadcast Services
P.O. Box 2310
Window Rock, AZ 86515

602 871-6656
Fax: 602 871-7355

Arizona Film Commission
3800 N. Central Avenue,
  Building D
Phoenix, AZ 85012

800 523-6695, 602 280-1380
Fax: 602 280-1384

Greater Flagstaff
  Economic Council
1515 E. Cedar Avenue, Suite B-1
Flagstaff, AZ 86004

602 799-7658
Fax: 602 556-0940

Lake Havasu Area Film Commission
1930 Mesquite Avenue, Suite 3
Lake Havasu City, AZ 86403

602-453-3456
Fax: 602 680-0010

Page/Lake Powell Film Commission
638 Elm Street
P.O Box 727
Page, AZ 86040

602 645-2741

City of Phoenix Motion Picture
  Office
251 W. Washington
Phoenix, AZ 85003

602 262-4850
Fax: 602 534-2295

Scottsdale Film Office
3939 Civic Center Boulevard
Scottsdale, AZ 85251

602 944-2636
Fax: 602 994-2641

Sedona Film Commission
P.O. Box 2489
Sedona, AZ 86336

602 204-1123

Tucson Film Office
32 N. Stone Avenue, Suite 100
Tucson, AZ 85701

Wickenburg Film Commission
P.O. Drawer CC
216 N. Frontier Street
Wickenburg, AZ 85385

602 684-5479
Fax: 602 684-5470

Yuma Film Commission
Yuma County Chamber of
  Commerce
P.O. Box 230
Yuma, AZ 85366

602 726-4027, 602 782-2567
Fax: 602 343-0038

## ARKANSAS

Arkansas Motion Picture
Development Office
1 State Capitol Mall, Room
2C-200
Little Rock, AR 72201

501 682-7676
Fax: 501 682-FILM

Chamber of Commerce/Eureka
Springs
P.O. Box 551
Eureka Springs, AR 72632

501 253-8738

## CALIFORNIA

California Film Commission
6922 Hollywood Boulevard,
Suite 600
Hollywood, CA 90028

213 736-2465
Fax: 213 736-3159

Big Bear Lake Film Commission
P.O. Box 2860
630 Bartlett Road
Big Bear Lake, CA 92315

714 866-6190
Fax: 714 866-5412

Eureka-Humboldt County Convention and Visitors Bureau
1034 2nd Street
Eureka, CA 95501

800 338-7352, 800 346-3482,
707 443-5097
Fax: 707 443-5115

Kern County Board of Trade/
Film Commission
P.O. Bin 1312
2101 Oak Street
Bakersfield, CA 93302

805 861-2367
Fax: 805 861-2017

Madera County Film Commis-
sion
P.O. Box 126
Bass Lake, CA 93604

209 642-3676
Fax: 209 642-2517

Monterey County Film Com-
mission
P.O. Box 111
Lighthouse Avenue
Monterey, CA 93940

408 646-0910
Fax: 408 655-9244

Oakland Film Commission
505 14th Street, Suite 715
Oakland, CA 94612

510 238-2193
Fax: 510 238-2227

Riverside County Film Commission
3499 10th Street
P.O. Box 1180
Riverside, CA 92502

714 788-9770
Fax: 714 788-1415

Sacramento Area Film Commission
1421 "K" Street
Sacramento, CA 95814

916 264-7777
Fax: 916 264-7788

San Diego Film Commission
402 W. Broadway, Suite 1000
San Diego, CA 92101-3585

619 234-3456
Fax: 619 234-0571

San Francisco Film and Video
Arts Commission
Mayor's Office
City Hall, Room 200
San Francisco, CA 94102

415 554-6244
Fax: 415 554-6160

San Jose Film and Video Commission
333 West San Carlos, Suite 1000
San Jose, CA 95110

800 726-5673, 408 295-9600
Fax: 408 295-3937

San Luis Obispo County Film
Commission
1041 Chorro Street, Suite E
San Luis Obispo, CA 93401

805 541-8000
Fax: 805 543-9498

Santa Barbara County Film
Commission
504 State Street
Santa Barbara, CA 93101

805 968-7356

Catalina Island Film Commission
P.O. Box 707
Avalon, CA 90704

310 510-2626
Fax: 310-510-1646

Palm Springs Desert Resorts
CVB
69-930 Highway 111, Suite 201
Rancho Mirage, CA 92270

619 770-9000
Fax: 619 770-9001

Santa Cruz County Conference
and Visitors Council
701 Front Street
Santa Cruz, CA 95060

408 425-1234
Fax: 408 425-1260

Santa Monica Mountains NRA
30401 Agoura Road, Suite 100
Agoura Hills, CA 91301

818 597-1036, X212
Fax: 818 597-8537

Sonoma County Film/Video
Commission
10 Fourth Street, Suite 100
Santa Rosa, CA 95401-6210

707 575-1191
Fax: 707 578-0555

Greater Stockton Chamber of
Commerce
445 W. Weber Avenue, Suite
220
Stockton, CA 95203

209 466-7066
Fax: 209 466-5271

## COLORADO

Colorado Motion Picture and
Television Commission
1625 Broadway, Suite 1975
Denver, CO 80202

303 572-5444
Fax: 303 572-5099

Bent's Fort Film Commission of
Southeastern Colorado
P.O. Box 487
Lincoln Square Building
Lajunta, CO 81050

719 384-7711
Fax: 719 384-8140

Boulder County Film Commission
2440 Pearl Street
P.O. Box 73
Boulder, CO 80306

800 444-0447, 303 442-1044
Fax: 303 938-8837

Canon City Chamber of Commerce
1032 Royal Gorge
Canon City, CO 81215-0749

719 275-5149

Colorado Springs Film Commission
30 S. Nevada Avenue, Suite 405
Colorado Springs, CO 80903

719 578-6279
Fax: 719 578-6394

Mayor's Office of Art, Culture
and Film
1445 Cleveland Place, Room
206
Denver, CO 80202

303 640-2678
Fax: 303 640-4627

Greeley/Weld County Film
Commission
1407 8th Avenue
Greeley, CO 80631

303 352-3566
Fax: 303 352-3572

Southwest Colorado Film Commission
108 Miller Student Center
Fort Lewis College
Durango, CO 81301

303 247-7169
Fax: 303 247-7620

Steamboat Springs/Yampa Valley Film Board
Box 772305
Steamboat Springs, CO 80477

303 879-0882
Fax: 303 879-2543

Trinidad Film Commission
309 Nevada Avenue
Trinidad, CO 81082

719 846-9412
Fax: 719 846-4550

Anasazi Film Commission
Ute Mountain/Ute Tribe
Mike Wash Road
P.O. Box 52
Towaoc, CO 81334

303 565-6485
Fax: 303 565-7412

## CONNECTICUT
Connecticut Film Commission
865 Brook Street
Rocky Hill, CT 06067-3405

203 258-4301
Fax: 203 563-4877

## DELAWARE
Delaware Development Office
99 Kings Highway
P.O. Box 1401

Dover, DE 19903

800 441-8846, 302 739-4271
Fax: 302 739-5749

## DISTRICT OF COLUMBIA
Mayor's Office of TV and Film
717 14th Street N.W., 10th
   Floor
Washington, DC 20005

202 727-6600
Fax: 202 727-3787

## FLORIDA
Florida Film Bureau
466 Collins Building
107 W. Gaines Street
Tallahassee, FL 32399-2000

904 487-1100
Fax: 904 922-5943

Space Coast Film Commission
C/O Brevard County Government Center
2725 St. Johns Street
Melbourne, FL 32940

800 USA-1969, 407 633-2110
Fax: 407 633-2112

Film and Television Office
Broward Economic Development
Council, Inc.
200 E. Las Olas Boulevard, Suite 1850
Ft. Lauderdale, FL 33301

305 524-3113
Fax: 305 524-3167

Clearwater Film Commission
P.O. Box 4748
Clearwater, FL 34618-4748

813 462-6893
Fax: 813 462-6720

Lee County Board of County
Commissioners—Film Liaison
Office
P.O. Box 398
Fort Myers, FL 33902

813 335-2685
Fax: 813 335-2961

Gainesville Area Chamber of
Commerce
300 E. University
Gainesville, FL 32601

904 336-7100
Fax: 904 336-7141

Jacksonville Film and TV Office
128 E. Forsyth Street, Suite 505
Jacksonville, FL 32202

904 630-1905
Fax: 904 630-1485

Florida Keys and Key West Film
Commission
402 Wall Street
P.O. Box 984
Key West, FL 33040

800 527-8539, 305 294-2587
Fax: 305 294-7806

Manatee County Film Commission
P.O. Box 1000
Bradenton, FL 34206

813 746-5989
Fax: 813 747-7459

Miami/Dade Office of Film and
Television
50 S.W. 32 Road, Building 9
Miami, FL 33130

305 372-3456
Fax: 305 579-2509

Ocala/Marion County Film
Commission
110 E. Silver Springs Boulevard
Ocala, FL 32670

800 476-9898, 904 629-2757
Fax: 904 629-1581

Orlando Film Office
200 E. Robinson Street, Suite 600
Orlando, FL 32801

407 422-7159
Fax: 407 843-9514

Palm Beach County Film Liaison Office
1555 Palm Beach Lakes Boulevard, Suite 204
West Palm Beach, FL 33401

407 233-1000
Fax: 407 471-3990

Motion Picture and Television Dept./Central Florida Dev. Council
P.O. Box 1839
600 N. Broadway, Suite 300
Bartow, FL 33830

813 534-4371
Fax: 813 533-1247

St. Lucie County Film Liaison Office
900 Virginia Avenue, Suite 16
Ft. Pierce, FL 34982

800 532-0099, 407 460-6700
Fax: 407 460-6701

## GEORGIA
Georgia Film and Videotape Office
285 Peachtree Center Avenue, Suite 1000
Atlanta, GA 30303

404 656-7830
Fax: 404 651-9063

City of Tampa Motion Picture and Television Development
306 E. Jackson
Tampa, FL 33602

813 223-8419
Fax: 813 227-7176

Volusia County Film Office Destination Daytona!
P.O. Box 910
126 E. Orange Avenue
Daytona Beach, FL 32115

800 854-1234, 904 255-0415
Fax: 904 255-5478

## HAWAII
Hawaii has a four-month quarantine. A plus for readers living in Hawaii, but a minus for all others.

Film Industry Branch
P.O. Box 2359
Honolulu, HI 96804

808 586-2570
Fax: 818 586-2572

Maui Motion Picture Coordination Committee
380 Dairy Road
P.O. Box 1738
Kahului, HI 96734

808 871-8691
Fax: 808 877-7560

## IDAHO
Idaho Film Bureau
700 W. State Street, 2nd Floor
Boise, ID 83702

800 942-8338, 208 334-2470
Fax: 208 334-2631

## ILLINOIS
Illinois Film Office
100 W. Randolph, Suite 3-400
Chicago, IL 60601

312 814-3600
Fax: 312 814-6732

Chicago Film Office
1 N. Lasalle, Suite 2165
Chicago, IL 60602

312 744-6415
Fax: 312 744-1378

Quad Cities Development
  Group/Film Coalition
1830 2nd Avenue, Suite 200
Rock Island, IL 61201

319 326-1005
Fax: 309 788-4964

## INDIANA
Indiana Tourism and Film
Development Division
Department of Commerce
1 N. Capitol
Indianapolis, IN 46204

317 232-8829
Fax: 317 232-8995

# IOWA
Iowa Film Office
Department of Economic
  Development
200 E. Grand Avenue
Des Moines, IA 50309

800 779-3456, 515 242-4726
Fax: 515 242-4859

Cedar Rapids Area Film Commission
P.O. Box 5339
119 First Avenue S.E.
Cedar Rapids, IA 52406-5339

800 735-5557, 319 398-5009
Fax: 319 398-5089

Fort Dodge Film Office
Mayor's Office
819 1st Avenue South
Fort Dodge, IA 50501

515 573-7144
Fax: 515 573-5097

Greater Des Moines Film Commission
601 Locust, Suite 222
Des Moines, IA 50309

800 451-2625, 515 286-4960
Fax: 515 244-9757

Dubuque Film Bureau
705 Town Clock Plaza
P.O. Box 705
Dubuque, IA 52004-0705

319 557-9200
Fax: 319 557-1591

# KANSAS
Kansas Film Commission
700 S.W. Harrison Street, Suite
  1300
Topeka, KS 66603

913 296-4927
Fax: 913 296-5055

Lawrence Convention and Visitors Bureau/Film Office
734 Vermont
Box 586
Lawrence, KS 66044

913 865-4411
Fax: 913 865-4400

Manhattan Film Commission
555 Poyntz, Suite 290
Manhattan, KS 66502

913 776-8829

Overland Park Film Commission
10975 Benson, Suite 360
Overland Park, KS 66210

913 491-0123
Fax: 913 491-0015

Topeka Convention and Visitors
   Bureau
3 Townsite Plaza
120 E. 6th Street, Suite 100
Topeka, KS 66603

800 235-1030, 913 234-1030
Fax: 913 234-8282

## KENTUCKY
Kentucky Film Office
500 Mero Street
Capitol Plaza Tower, 22nd Floor
Frankfort, KY 40601

800 345-6591, 502 564-3456
Fax: 502 564-7588

## LOUISIANA
Louisiana Film Commission
P.O. Box 44320
Baton Rouge, LA 70804-4320

504 342-8150
Fax: 504 342-7988

Jeff Davis Parish Film Commis-
   sion
P.O. Box 1207
Jennings, LA 70546

318 821-5534
Fax: 318 821-5536

## MAINE
Maine Film Office
State House Station 59
Augusta, ME 04333

207 289-5707
Fax: 207 289-2861

Wichita Convention and Visitors Bureau
100 S. Main, Suite 100
Wichita, KS 67202

316 265-2800
Fax: 316 265-0162

New Orleans Film Commission
1300 Perdido
City Hall/Room 2W17
New Orleans, LA 70112

504 565-6580
Fax: 504 565-6588

## MARYLAND

Maryland Film Commission
601 N. Howard Street
Baltimore, MD 21201

410 333-6633
Fax: 410 333-1062

Baltimore Film Commission
303 E. Fayette, Suite 300
Baltimore, MD 21202

410 396-4550
Fax: 410 727-5850

## MASSACHUSETTS

Massachusetts Film Office
10 Park Plaza, Suite 2310
Boston, MA 02116

617 973-8800
Fax: 617 973-8810

## MICHIGAN

Michigan Film Office
P.O. Box 30004
Lansing, MI 48909

800 477-FILM, 517 373-0638
Fax: 517 343-3872

## MINNESOTA

Minnesota Film Board
401 N. 3rd Street, Suite 401
Minneapolis, MN 55401

612 332-6493
Fax: 612 332-3735

## MISSISSIPPI

Mississippi Film Office:
1200 Walter Sillers Building:
Box 849
Jackson, MS 39205

601 359-3297
Fax: 601 359-2832

Prince George's County Media/
    Film Office
9475 Loftsford Road, Suite 125
Landover, MD 20785

301 386-3456, 301 577-5785
Fax: 301 322-6132

Mayor's Office of Film/TV
126 City/County Building
Detroit, MI 48226

313 224-4733
Fax: 313 224-7157

Columbus Film Commission
P.O. Box 789
Columbus, MS 39703

800 327-2686, 601 329-1191
Fax: 601 327-3417

Mississippi Gulf Coast
Film Office/Harrison County
   Dev. Commission
P.O. Box 569
Gulfport, MS 39502

601 863-3807
Fax: 601 863-4555

Oxford Film Commission
P.O. Box 965
Oxford, MS 38655

601 234-4651
Fax: 601 234-4655

## MISSOURI
Missouri Film Office
P.O. Box 1055
301 W. High
Jefferson City, MO 65102

314 751-9050
Fax: 314 751-5160

Greater Kansas City Film Commission
920 Main Street, 6th Floor
Kansas City, MO 64105

816 221-2424
Fax: 816 221-7440

## MONTANA
Montana Film Office
1424 9th Avenue
Helena, MT 59620

800 548-3390, 406 444-2654
Fax: 406 444-2808

Tupelo Film Commission
P.O. Box 1485
Tupelo, MS 38802-1485

800 533-0611, 601 841-6521
Fax: 601 841-6558

Vicksburg Film Commission
P.O. Box 110
Vicksburg, MS 39180

800 221-3536, 601 636-9421
Fax: 601 636-9475

St. Louis Film Partnership
100 S. 4th Street, Suite 500
St. Louis, MO 63102

314 231-5555, 314 444-1174
Fax: 314 444-1122

Northern Montana Film Com-
   mission
P.O. Box 2127
Railroad Square Express Build-
   ing, 2nd Floor
Great Falls, MT 59403

800 735-8535
Fax: 406 453-5000

## NEBRASKA
Nebraska Film Office
P.O. Box 94666
301 Centennial Mall South
Lincoln, NE 68509-4666

800 228-4307, 402 471-3368
Fax: 402 471-3778

## NEVADA
Omaha/Douglas County Film
  Commission
1819 Farnam Street, Suite 1206
Omaha, NE 68163

402 444-7736, 402 444-7737
Fax: 402 444-4511

Motion Picture Division Commission on Economic Dev.
3770 Howard Hughes Parkway,
Suite 925
Las Vegas, NV 89158

702 486-7150
Fax: 702 486-7372

Robin Holabird
5151 S. Carson Street
Carson City, NV 89710

702 687-4325
Fax: 702 687-4450

## NEW HAMPSHIRE
New Hampshire Film and TV
  Bureau
172 Pembroke Road
P.O. Box 856
Concord, NH 03302-0856

603 271-2598, X108
Fax: 603 271-2629

## NEW JERSEY
New Jersey Motion Picture and
  Television Commission
P.O. Box 47028
153 Halsey Street
Newark, NJ 07101

201 648-6279
Fax: 201 648-7350

## NEW MEXICO

New Mexico Film Commission
1050 Pecos Trail
Santa Fe, NM 87501

800 545-9871, 505 827-7365
Fax: 505 827-7369

Albuquerque Film/TV Commission
P.O. Box 1293
Old City Hall
Albuquerque, NM 87103

505 768-4512
Fax: 505 768-3967

Las Cruces Convention and Visitors Bureau
311 N. Downtown Mall
Las Cruces, NM 88001

800 FIESTAS, 505 524-8521
Fax: 505 526-7212

City of Tucumcari
P.O. Box 1188
215 E. Center
Tucumcari, NM 88401

505 461-3451
Fax: 505 461-0418

## NEW YORK

New York State Governor's
Office for MP/TV
Development
Pier 62
W. 23rd Street and Hudson
River
New York, NY 10011

212 929-0240
Fax: 212 929-0506

New York City Office of Film/
Theatre/Broadcasting
254 W. 54th Street, 13th Floor
New York, NY 10019

212 489-6710
Fax: 212 307-6237

Rochester/Finger Lakes
Film and Video Office
126 Andrews Street
Rochester, NY 14604-1102

716 546-5490
Fax: 716 232-4822

## NORTH CAROLINA

North Carolina Film Office
430 N. Salisbury Street
Raleigh, NC 27611

800 232-9227, 919 733-9900
Fax: 919 715-0151

Asheville Convention and Visitors Bureau
P.O. Box 1010
Asheville, NC 28802

704 258-6121
Fax: 704 251-0926

Winston-Salem Film Commission
601 W. 4th Street
Winston-Salem, NC 67101

800 331-7018, 919 725-2361
Fax: 919 773-1404

## NORTH DAKOTA
North Dakota Film
  Commission
604 East Boulevard
Bismarck, ND 58505

800 435-5663, 701 224-2525
Fax: 701 224-4878

## OHIO
Ohio Film Bureau
77 S. High Street, 29th Floor
P.O. Box 1001
Columbus, OH 43266-0101

800 848-1300, 614 466-2284
Fax: 614 466-6744

## OKLAHOMA
Oklahoma Film Office
440 S. Houston, Room 505
Tulsa, OK 74127

800 766-3456, 913 581-2806
Fax: 918 581-2844

Lawton Film Commission
P.O. Box 1376
Lawton, OK 73502

800 872-4540, 405 355-3541
Fax: 405 357-3642

## OREGON
Oregon Film Office
775 Summer Street N.E.
Salem, OR 97310

503 373-1232
Fax: 503 581-5115

City Manager's Office
P.O. Box 1810
Wilmington, NC 28604

919 341-7810
Fax: 919 341-7887

Greater Cincinnati Film Commission
435 Elm Street
Cincinnati, OH 45202

513 784-1744
Fax: 513 768-8963

Tulsa Convention/Visitors Bureau
616 S. Boston
Tulsa, OK 74119

913 585-1201
Fax: 918 585-8386

## PENNSYLVANIA

Pennsylvania Film Bureau
Forum Building, Room 449
Harrisburg, PA 17120

717 783-3456
Fax: 717 234-4560

Greater Philadelphia Film Office
1650 Arch Street, 19th Floor
Philadelphia, PA 19103

215 686-2668
Fax: 215 686-3659

Pittsburgh Film Office
Benedum Trees Building, Suite
  1300
Pittsburgh, PA 15222

412 261-2744
Fax: 412 471-7317

## PUERTO RICO

Puerto Rico Film Commission
P.O. Box 362350
San Juan, PR 00936-2350

819 758-4747, 809 754-7110
Fax: 809 754-9645

Puerto Rico Film Commission
1901 Avenue of the Stars, Suite
  1774
Los Angeles, CA 90067

310 788-0722
Fax: 310 788-0723

## SOUTH CAROLINA

South Carolina Film Office
P.O. Box 927
Columbia, SC 29202

803 737-0490
Fax: 803 737-0418

## SOUTH DAKOTA

South Dakota Film Commission
711 East Wells Avenue
Pierre, SD 57501-3369

800 952-3625, 605 773-3301
Fax: 605 773-3256

## TENNESSEE

Tennessee Film
  Entertainment/Music
  Commission
320 6th Avenue North, 7th
Floor
Nashville, TN 37219

800 251-8594, 615 741-3456
Fax: 615 741-5829

## TEXAS

Texas Film Commission
P.O. Box 13246
Austin, TX 78711

512 469-9111
Fax: 512 320-9569

Amarillo Film Office
1000 S. Polk Street
Amarillo, TX 79101

800 692-1338, 806 374-1497
Fax: 806 373-3909

Film Commission of North
  Texas
3 Dallas Communications Complex
6311 N. O'Connor Road, Suite
  N57-LB57
Irving, TX 75039

214 869-7657
Fax: 214 869-1582

Irving Texas Film Commission
6311 N. O'Connor Road
L.B. 119
Irving, TX 75039

800 2-IRVING, 214 869-0303
Fax: 214 869-4609

Memphis/Shelby County
  Film Tape/Music Commis-
  sion
Beale Street Landing
245 Wagner Place, Suite 4
Memphis, TN 38103-3815

901 527-8300
Fax: 901 527-8326

El Paso Film Commission
1 Civic Center Plaza
El Paso, TX 79901

800 351-6024, 915 534-0698
Fax: 915 532-2963

Houston Film Commission
3300 Main Street
Houston, TX 77002

800 231-7799, 713 523-5050
Fax: 713 524-5376

San Antonio Convention and
  Visitors Bureau
P.O. Box 2277
San Antonio, TX 78298

800 447-3372, X730; 512 270-
  8700
Fax: 512 270-8782

## U.S. VIRGIN ISLANDS
U.S. Virgin Islands Film
  Promotion Office
P.O. Box 6400
St. Thomas, VI 00804

809 775-1444, 809 774-8784
Fax: 809 774-4390

## UTAH
Utah Film Commission
324 S. State Street, Suite 500
Salt Lake City, UT 84111

800 453-8824, 801 538-8740
Fax: 801 538-8886

Central Utah Film Commission
51 S. University Avenue, Suite
  110
Provo, UT 84606

800 222-8824, 801 371-8390
Fax: 801 370-8050

Moab Film Commission
59 S. Main, Suite 4
Moab, UT 84532

801 259-6388, 801 259-7809
Fax: 801 259-6399

Park City Film Commission
P.O. Box 1630
Park City, UT 84060

800 453-1360, 801 649-6100
Fax: 801 649-4132

Washington County Travel/
  Conv/Film Office

425 S. 700 East
The Dixie Center
St. George, UT 84770

800 869-6635, 801 634-5747
Fax: 801 628-1619

## VERMONT
Vermont Film Bureau
134 State Street
Montpelier, VT 05602

802 828-3236, 802 828-3230
Fax: 802 828-3233

## VIRGINIA
Virginia Film Office
P.O. Box 798
1021 E. Cary Street
Richmond, VA 23206-0798

804 371-8204
Fax: 804 786-1121

Metro Richmond Convention
and Visitors Bureau
300 E. Main Street, Suite 100
Richmond, VA 23219

804 782-2777
Fax: 804 780-2577

## WASHINGTON
Washington State Film and
Video Office
2001 6th Avenue, Suite 2700
Seattle, WA 98121

206 464-7148
Fax: 206 464-5868

City of Tacoma/Film Production
747 Market Street, Suite 243
Tacoma, WA 98402

206 591-5790
Fax: 206 591-5300

## WEST VIRGINIA
West Virginia Film Industry
Development Office
2101 Washington Street East
Charleston, WV 25305

800 225-5982, 304 558-2286
Fax: 304 558-0108

## WISCONSIN
Wisconsin Film Office
123 W. Washington, 6th Floor
Box 7970
Madison, WI 53707

608 267-3456
Fax: 608 266-3403

City of Milwaukee Film Liaison
809 N. Broadway
Milwaukee, WI 53202

414 223-5818
Fax: 414 223-5904

## WYOMING
Wyoming Film Commission
I-25 and College Drive
Cheyenne, WY 82002-0240

800 458-6657, 307 777-7777
Fax: 307 777-6904

Jackson Hole Film Commission
P.O. Box E
Jackson, WY 83001

307 733-3316
Fax: 307 733-5585

Northwest Wyoming/Park
  County Film Commission
109 W. Yellowstone
Cody, WY 82414

307 587-6074
Fax: 307 527-7640

Sheridan County Film Promotion
150 S. Main
Sheridan, WY 82818

307 672-2481
Fax: 307 672-8107

# ★ INTERNATIONAL

Why are we listing foreign countries? Some of the foreign film commissioners can help you if you are planning an extended visit to their country and want to get paid while there. Contact them at least six months in advance, but make your travel reservations at the last minute because films have a tendency to be canceled or have their starting date adjusted at the eleventh hour. You will need a work permit in your destination and veterinarian certificates and travel permits for your pet. Local requirements can be obtained from the country's nearest consulate or embassy, but you have the added advantage of having a new friend to pave the way for you, the film commissioner.

## AUSTRALIA

There is a six-month quarantine in Australia. Check current regulations.

New South Wales Film and
  Television Office
Levvell 6, 1 Francis Street
Sydney, NSW
2010
Australia

61 2 380-5599
Fax: 61 2 360-1090

Queensland Pacific Film and
  Television Commission
100 George Street, 4th Floor
Brisbane, Queensland
4000
Australia

61 7 224-4114
Fax: 61 7 229-7538

Western Australian Film Council
336 Churchill Avenue, Suite 8
Subiaco, Western Australia
6008
Australia

61 9 382-2500
Fax: 61 9 381-2848

## AUSTRIA
Cineaustria
11601 Wilshire Boulevard, Suite
2480
Los Angeles, CA 90025

310 477-3332
Fax: 310 477-5141

## BAHAMAS
Bahamas Film Promotion
Bureau
P.O. Box N 3701
Nassau, Bahamas

809 326-0635, 809 322-8634
Fax: 809 328-0945

Bahamas Film Promotion/Miami
255 Alhambra Circle, Suite 414
Coral Gables, FL 33134

305 444-8428
Fax: 305 444-1080

## CANADA
Alberta Economic Development
and Trade
9940 106th Street
Sterling Place
Edmonton, AB T5K 2P6
Canada

403 427-2005
Fax: 403 427-5924

Calgary Film Services
P.O. Box 2100
Station M
Calgary, AB T2P 2MS
Canada

403 268-2771
Fax: 403 268-1946

Edmonton Motion Picture and
Television Bureau
9797 Jasper Avenue
Edmonton, AB T5J 1N9
Canada

800 661-6965, 403 424-7870
Fax: 403 426-0535

British Columbia Film Commission
601 W. Cordova Street
Vancouver, BC V6B 1G1
Canada

604 660-2732
Fax: 604 660-4790

Burnaby Film Office
4949 Canada Way
Burnaby BC V5G 1M2
Canada

604 294-7231
Fax: 604 294-7220

Thompson-Nicola Film Com-
mission
2079 Falcon Road
Kamloops, BC V2C4J2
Canada

604 372-9336, 604 573-4671
Fax: 604 372-5048

Victoria/Vancouver Island Film
Commission
525 Fort Street
Victoria, BC V8W 1E8
Canada

604 386-3976
Fax: 604 385-3552

Location Manitoba
333-93 Lombard Avenue
Winnipeg, MB 43B 3B1
Canada

204 947-2040
Fax: 204 956-5261

New Brunswick Film/Video
Commission
P.O.Box 6000
Fredericton, NB E3B 5H1
Canada

506 453-2553
Fax: 506 453-2416

Nova Scotia Film Development
Corporation
1724 Granville Street
Halifax, NS B3J 1X5
Canada

902 424-7185
Fax: 902 424-0563

Ontario Film Development
Corp.
175 Bloor Street East, Suite 300,
North Tower
Toronto, ONT M4W 3R8
Canada

416 314-6858, 213 621-2070
Fax: 416 314-6876

Toronto Film Liaison Planning
and Development
The Corporation of the City of
Toronto
20th Floor, E Tower
City Hall
Toronto, ONT M5H 2N2
Canada

416 392-7570
Fax: 416 392-0675

Quebec Government Film and
TV Office
1755 E. Rene-Levesque Boule-
vard, Suite 200
Montreal, QB H2K 4P6
Canada

514 873-5027, 514 873-7768
Fax: 514 873-4388

Montreal Film Commission
425 Place Jacques Cartier, Suite
300
Montreal, QB H2K 4P6
Canada

514 873-5027, 514 873-7768
Fax: 514 873-4388

Quebec City Film Bureau
399 St. Joseph Street East, 2nd
Floor
Quebec City, QB G1K 8E2
Canada

418 648-0965, 418 691-7538
Fax: 418 529-3121

## FRANCE
South of France Film
Commission
Rue Emile Miramont
83570 Entrecasteaux
France

33 94-04-4070
Fax: 33 94-04-4998

Saskfilm
1840 McIntyre Street, 2nd Floor
Regina, SASK S4P 2P9
Canada

306 347-3456
Fax: 306 359-7768

City of Regina/Director of Pub-
lic Affairs
P.O. Box 1790
Regina, SASK SP 3C8
Canada

306 777-7486
Fax: 306 777-6803

Yukon Film Promotion Office
P.O. Box 2703
Whitehorse, YK 61A 2C6
Canada

403 667-5400
Fax: 403 667-2634

## GERMANY

German Film Commission
C/O Filmstiftung
Nordrhein-Westfalen GMBH
Palmenstrasse 16
2000 Düsseldorf
Nordrhein-Westfalen
Germany

49 211-93-3030
Fax: 49 211-93-3033

Munich Film Information Office
Kaiserstrasse 39
D-8000 München 40
Germany

49 89-381-90432, 49 89-381-90433
Fax: 49 89-381-90426

## GUATEMALA

Guatemala Tourist Commission
7A. Avenida 1-17 Zona 4,
    Centro Civico
Guatemala City
Guatemala

502 231-1333
Fax: 502 231-8893

## HONG KONG

Hong Kong Film Liaison
10940 Wilshire Boulevard, Suite
    1220
Los Angeles, CA 90024
310 208-2678
Fax: 310 208-1869

## ISRAEL

Israel Film Centre
30 Agron Street
Jerusalem
Israel

972 2-210111, 213 658-7924
Fax: 972 2-245110

## JAMAICA
Jamaica Film Office
35 Trafalgar Road, 3rd Floor
Kingston 10
Jamaica

809 929-9450, 809 926-4613
Fax: 809 924-9650

## MALTA
Malta Investment Mgmt.
  Company, Ltd.
Trade Center
San Gwann Industrial Estate
Birkirkara, SGN 09
Malta

356 496-523, 356 44-97-801
Fax: 356 499-568

## MEXICO
Consejo Estatal de Cine Teatro
  y TV
Rufino Tamayo 4, Co.
  Acapantzingo
Cuernavaca, Morales 62440
Mexico

52 73-129071
Fax: 52 73-143654

## NORWAY
Scanfilms Norway
Mediesenteret
Fossetunet 3
P.O. Box 191
N-5801 Sogndal
Norway

47 56-73059
Fax: 47 56-76190

## POLAND
Ampol-Poland Film/TV Liaison
14814 Sunset Boulevard
Pacific Palisades, CA 90272

310 573-1815
Fax: 310 454-6575

## SPAIN
Catalonia Film Commission
Alicante, 27-3RD F
Barcelona
Spain 08022

34 3 418-2206, 34 3 417-9551
Fax: 34 3 418-2205

Madrid Audiovisual/Instituto
  Madrileno de Desarrollo
Garcia de Paredes, 92
E-28010 Madrid
Spain

34 1 410-2063
Fax; 34 1 319-4290

## THAILAND
Thailand Film Promotion
  Center
599 Bumrung Muang Road
Bangkok 10100
Thailand

66 2 223-4690, 66 2 223-4475
Fax: 66 2 223-2586

## ENGLAND
There is a six-month quarantine of warm-blooded animals
in England.

British Film Commission
70 Baker Street
London WIM ADJ
England

44 71 224-5000
Fax: 44 71 224-1013

## BRITISH VIRGIN ISLANDS
Check current quarantine regulations.

British Virgin Islands Film
  Commission
Office of the Chief Minister
Government of the British Virgin
  Islands
Road Town, Tortola
British Virgin Islands

809 494-3701
Fax: 809 494-6413

Birmingham Media Develop-
  ment Agency
The Bond
180-182 Fazeley Street
Digbeth
Birmingham B5 5SE
England

44 21 766-8899
Fax: 44 21 766-8988

Isle of Man Film Commission
  Department of Tourism
Sea Terminal Buildings
Douglas
Isle of Man
44 0624-686841
Fax: 44 0624-686800

Liverpool Film Office
William Brown Street
Central Libraries
Liverpool L3 8EW
England

44 51 225-5446
Fax: 44 51 207-1342

## SCOTLAND
There is a six-month quarantine.

Scottish Screen Locations
Filmhouse, 88 Lothian Road
Edinburgh EH3 9BZ
Scotland

44 31 229-1213
Fax: 44 31 229-1070

Edinburgh and Lothian Screen
  Industries Office
Filmhouse, 88 Lothian Road
Edinburgh, EH3 9BZ
Scotland

44 31 228-5960
Fax: 44-31 228-5967

## **WALES**

There is a six-month quarantine.

Gwynedd County Council
County Offices
Caernarvon, Gwynedd LL551SH
Wales

44 02 86-679673
Fax: 44 0286-78495

# APPENDIX 2

# Tricks of the Trade

> "I'm afraid the public knows me too well. They know every shade of voice, every trick, every god-damned movement I can make."
>
> **Sir Laurence Olivier**

1. Shoot rehearsals. Film, while expensive, is the cheapest commodity on the set. Waste a little film to insure that the perfect performance in rehearsal is not wasted.

2. Do not use spray makeup on cats. They will immediately start licking it off.

3. Dog, cat, bird, lizard, snake should be able to move at two speeds *minimum:* slow and fast. If you can get a medium in there too, that's fine.

4. Use two handlers, both off camera. One to hold the animal in the stand position and the other to call the animal.

5. If you have loose birds and you're trying to get them on a sound stage, shut off all the lights, except in one brightly lit room. They'll fly to the light.

6. If you are working with bats (lucky you: boy, are they strange pets!), the reverse of the above is true.

**7.** To give a silent signal, use the Captain Haggerty Key Light Cuing System. See page 172 for a full discussion.

**8.** Always try to use pure-bred animals. They are easier to match for backup animals or at sometime in the future.

**9.** Keep the hair out of the eyes of animals when working them. They are less likely to spook or shy away.

**10.** Courtesy dictates that when working on a film you offer to give the sound man a wild track of your dog barking, cat meowing, pig oinking, cow mooing.

**11.** When offering to give the sound man a wild track, pick a time (a) when everything is quiet on the set; (b) no shooting is taking place; (c) when both you and sound are not busy; and (d) before you are dismissed for the day. If necessary, move to another area to get the desired sound.

**12.** If your animal has been ready for the shot for some time, or if you are concerned that the sound of the clapper will throw your placid pet off, call for a tail slate, or end slate (see Glossary for definition).

**13.** If you are asked if your animal can do the assignment in one take, tell them, "Sure! Can your people shoot it in one take?"

**14.** Logging individual takes is a good idea, if you have extra personnel on the set. Unobtrusively note scene and take number and the reason the take was not successful. This will accomplish three things: (a) It will teach you a lot about the film business regarding directing, editing, shooting, sound, etc. (Remember—

this is an on-going education); (b) it will let you know just how professional your precious pet is; (c) if someone blames your animal for ruining a shot, you can recite exactly what the problems were on each shot.

15. Never be reluctant to request anything that you need for your animal's safety or comfort.

16. Keep that cat lean and mean! Cats have a tendency, particularly those with overindulgent owners, to pack on the poundage. Fat cats are great cats but also very lazy. It is tough to get work out of them. Weigh and measure your fabulous feline's food intake.

17. Do duplicate your darling dolphin's dulcet tones. Who better than you can imitate your pet? With practice you can do a credible imitation that will be more than adequate for any sound take.

18. Once the production company becomes locked in on something (location, animal, actor, cinematographer, etc.), even the hounds of hell will not change it.

19. Regarding the above: It isn't easy to determine when they are locked in on something, and everything is subject to change.

20. Always plan on a backup—backup animal, handler, vehicle, or whatever it takes to have the job done.

21. Make it look easy. That is the true sign of the pro. Complaining about how difficult your job is, is wrong. Subtle bragging about your professionalism is okay.

22. If a backup animal is requested, charge them for it. If you have one to spare, bring it along if it's no problem.

Don't forget to tell them what a great deal you are giving them.

23. When billing, write down everything you supplied. Let them know what they are getting for their price. If you have given them an unrequested backup animal, write "no charge." Everybody likes a deal, particularly in show Business.

24. Prepare a kit to take with you. If you used it once before, you might need it again. Get a good-quality, lightweight sturdy carrier with your name painted on it. It pays to advertise.

25. Learn as much as you can about the other theatrical crafts. Even take courses if necessary.

26. "Hypnotize" birds to calm them down on the set. Tuck a bird's head under its wings and rotate the bird. Birds will be calm and relaxed when they are placed down and they take their heads out from under their wings.

27. Reptiles and amphibians can be controlled by cooling them off to slow them down and by keeping them warm to increase their activity.

28. If, when quoting a price, you are told that they are going to give you a lot of work in the future, you can bet your last dollar they will never call you again, even though you gave them a good deal.

29. When submitting your bill, give them information as to how the credit should read.

30. Pay more attention to your gut feelings than what logic tells you.

**31.** They will never shoot it the way you visualized it, so make sure your animal can do it many different ways.

**32.** Do not be afraid to offer suggestions as to how to shoot any scene your animal appears in.

**33.** Break the performance down into parts and train your pet to do each of the parts individually. You'll combine all the training at the appropriate time.

**34.** Make your animal perform the exercise properly before finishing a training session.

**35.** Frogs should be transported with a wet burlap bag folded loosely around each of them and in a container with one to two inches of water in the bottom.

**36.** If your frog has to come out of the container jumping, warm it to 80 to 82 degrees. Chill it to keep it calm and placid.

**37.** It is necessary to transport animals in a safe, comfortable environment so they will be ready and able to perform.

**38.** Mammals, in particular, should be transported in equipment that is acceptable to onlookers. It is poor public relations to transport a domesticated animal any other way.

**39.** Worms and other forms of lower animal life can have their activity levels regulated by the amount of heat and cold. Test the amount of heat and exposure time *prior* to going to the studio. See how long their response time is.

**40.** Crickets should not be transported with standing water in their carrier or they will drown. Instead, put moistened cotton or paper toweling in the carrier.

**41.** The difference between a millipede and a centipede is that the millipede has *two* pairs of legs per body segment to the centipede's *one* pair.

**42.** Wash your hands after handling centipedes. Their bodies secrete toxins that can adversely affect open cuts and the mucous membranes.

**43.** Make sure that no actor or anyone else with an allergy handles poisonous or biting insects. While they may have little or no effect on the average person, they can be fatal to someone with allergies.

**44.** Do not release any animal into the wild. You do not know how it will affect the environment. You also do not know if that animal can survive in the wild.

**45.** When transporting a Rankins dragon, you should have a section in its carrier where the temperature is maintained at 90 degrees. It should have the option of leaving that 90-degree area.

**46.** Don't wear socks with holes in them when going on a job. Don't embarrass yourself, your mother and me.

**47.** Find out before going on the job if they are going to be using snow, fog or rain in the animal scenes. Here's why: (a) In the picturesque winter photograph of Saint Bernards and Siberian Huskies, there is a major problem. Artificial snow! Actors and models can control themselves and ignore the itching artificial snow falling down their backs, but it is impossible to explain that to a dog or cat. The problem can be overcome by having the snow fall in front of and behind the dog or cat rather than on them. Spraying a little artificial snow on your pet's coat will suffice for the "fallen snow" effect. (b) Fog, a staple of music videos and mystery and horror films, has an odor that is offensive to animals. Some fog material leaves a very greasy film on the floor, which is a safety hazard. (c) Rain, if falling on a dog, will cause inopportune shaking. A cat, as well as some other animals, will not tolerate it. The trick is to have the rain falling in front of *and* behind the animal.

**48.** Rather than having an actor handle two dogs on two leashes, put them both on the same leash and the dogs will do what the actor is incapable of doing.

**49.** With large carnivores, use the "cat chain" properly. Grasp the end ring and lay the chain, in small segments, across the upward-facing palm of the hand holding the ring. To test if you are handling the cat chain properly, pull it out of your hand without having the chain twist around your hand.

**50.** In handling large carnivores, the assistant handler should precede the animal and its handler carrying a wooden cane. The cane is to guide cast and crew out of the path of the animal by touching them on the lower portion of their legs, while announcing, "Lion coming through." The cane can also be used in emergency situations.

**51.** Do not wear jewelry, rings, earrings, etc., when handling animals. Besides distracting the animal, there is danger of having the jewelry catch on something.

**52.** Don't wear makeup, after-shave or perfume when working with exotics.

**53.** It is imperative when working with dangerous animals to have co-workers who will help you when the chips are down. Unfortunately, the only way you can *really* determine who will help you is when it is too late.

**54.** From day one, start building your theatrical kit. Keep adding everything you need for your pet.

# ★ THE CAPTAIN HAGGERTY KEY LIGHT CUING SYSTEM

The purpose of the key lighting cue is to give directions/commands to your animal. Work this out with the gaffer beforehand. The gaffer will clear it with the director or assistant director if necessary. The cue can be used for visual or voice signals, but it is best for visual signals. When on a lighted set, it is difficult to see beyond the set because everything is in darkness in comparison. A key light can be placed on the animal handler (you), who is off the set, so that the handler can be seen by the animal. The light can be turned on at the split second the signal is to be given to the animal. It is a cue for the animal handler to signal the animal. Under certain circumstances the light can be kept on if the handler determines that a constant contact should be maintained with the animal.

## Further Considerations and Explanations

The reason that you check with the gaffer is to make sure that the balance of light on the set is not upset by this off-set lighting. In any event the gaffer has to place the light. This especially is easy to do in a TV studio because of the overabundance of lights.

*Where* the animal is looking is critical. This is something that you should be aware of continually. Nothing is more disconcerting than having an animal looking in the wrong direction because that is where the handler is positioned. *Your* location is important in the end product. The director may not notice. The cameraman may not notice. The editor may not notice. The viewers of the final product *will* notice. This is when people decided if you have done a really professional job.

In giving cues you must be aware of your animal's response time and give the cue the millisecond before your pet performs.

# APPENDIX 3

# Glossary

The second language of show Business is Yiddish. If you don't believe me, read Neal Gabler's *An Empire of Their Own: How the Jews Invented Hollywood*. A selection of Yiddishisms, useful in show Business, is included in this glossary. Pronunciation is, at best, difficult. A universal cop-out, if someone criticizes your pronunciation, is to ask them what Yiddish accent they are using. This may confuse them. If they can't give you an answer, tell them your pronunciation is Litvak. If they say they are Litvak, tell them the pronunciation is Sephardic. You'll dazzle them with your footwork. The most critical pronunciation is the *ch* sound, which is like the clearing of your throat. Try the *ch* sound in the Scottish word "loch." Get that sound even approximately right and you will receive smiles of admiration for your knowledge of Yiddish. Most people are reluctant to even attempt it. For additional help with Yiddish, read anything on the subject by Leo Rosten.

**ABOVE-LINE COSTS** Costs established before the film goes into production, including the cost of the property, screenplay and creative personnel, such as producer director and star(s). Lower-level actors would be in the *below-line costs.*

**ADR** See *Automatic dialogue replacement.*

**AMBIANT SOUND** The sound of the surrounding area. This is very important for the final mix, so *keep quiet!* The sound is used to blend in or lie behind dialogue so that it doesn't come in with a hollow sound.

**AMBIANT TEMPERATURE** For your purposes the temperature in the area containing the animal must be monitored. This is important and in some cases may be critical. Be constantly aware of fluctuations in temperature on sets and locations. There are hot lights on sets, and air-conditioning cannot be used at all times because the sound of the equipment can be picked up. Activity levels, particularly in the case of herps (reptiles) can be controlled by temperature.

**ANIMAL AGENCY** A firm that books animal talent. Actually, it's not a true agency but a "packager" that puts all the animal work together. It has overhead, such as animal liability insurance, that a human agent would not have.

**ART DIRECTOR** The person in charge of the overall look of a project. Sometimes referred to as the production designer, the art director has a complete knowledge of all phases of the industry and is an artist in his own right. Each project has a characteristic, integrated appearance, and the art director creates and pulls it all together. Essentially a new world is created on each job, and the art director must control that with sets, color, lighting, wardrobe, props, locations and, very importantly, animals.

**ATMOSPHERE** (1) See *Extras;* (2) the overall appearance and ambiance of either a scene or an entire film created by technical means.

**AUTEUR THEORY** A theory that says a director is the auteur (French for author) who brings to the film not only a high professional competence but also his own style and personality. The auteur brings to the work an interior meaning which may not have been the intention of the original creator of the work.

**AUTOMATIC DIALOGUE REPLACEMENT** You will never be called in for this, but if you are, charge. It is the recording and re-recording of dialogue at a separate session in order to get it just right.

**BACKGROUND** See *Extras.*

**BAITING** A technique used to get an animal to perform in a certain way. Similar to *food reward* (which see), but with a slight variation, in that the food is seldom given completely. The best example of this is a show dog being baited by its handler to show an alert, rigid look. It enhances the dog's demeanor and appearance. Go to a dog show and see how this is done. See *Luring.*

**BEAT** As in "take a beat." A momentary pause before the animal executes its behavior.

**BEHAVIORS** Generally means training exercises or patterns that are taught to an animal. Different from "behavior." The singular of behaviors would be "a behavior," a term I detest because animals should be trained, not exhibiting behaviors.

**BELOW-LINE COSTS** Costs after the film has begun, including the costs of animal actors. These costs are for actual shooting and production of the film, such as cast and crew, film, equipment, editing, etc.

**BEST BOY** Gaffer's assistant.

**BOARD** See *Story board.*

**BOBBE-MYSEH** Yiddish. An old wives' tale, a fairy tale.

**BROCHE** Yiddish, with a clearing of the throat on the *ch*. A prayer, a blessing.

**BUBKES** Yiddish. (1) A trifle, insignificant, almost worthless; (2) absurd, foolish. "I come here with my superstar animal and you offer me *bubkes*." Pronounced with a long U (*oo*).

**CAMERA RIGHT OR LEFT** A direction that will be given to you and you *must* be aware of it. It is to the right or left of the camera as the camera faces you.

**CHANNELIZING** This has nothing to do with Shirley MacLaine. It is guiding the direction of an animal's movement with boundaries on either side. The boundaries can be very real, such as a long hallway, or they can be less clearly defined by equipment, lights, props, furniture, etc., on either side. Animals must return the same way as they have traveled when there is a retake of the scene. They should not be shown that there is another exit because they will take it.

**CLAPPER** The boards that are photographed at the beginning of a take listing director, cameraman, production, scene and take numbers. Clapping the hinged stick on the top gives a characteristic sound that is used to synchronize the film sound with the action. There are a number of other terms used for the item, the most common of which is *slate*.

**CLAPPER LOADER** The second assistant cameraman. This term is used primarily outside the United States. At one time, this was the way you could tell if a film was made outside the U.S.A. The term is being used more frequently in the States.

**CLIENT** The firm that has employed the services of an advertising agency to handle its account. A client is one step below God. If you work for the advertising agency, you realize that a client is one step *above* God.

**CONTINUITY**   For your purposes, it means keeping everything in order. If three days later you are continuing a scene in which the dog was on the actor's left side and the bird was perched on the actor's right hand, we cannot switch them. There are continuity people who are responsible for this, but as a pro you are also responsible for keeping things straight.

**CREDITS**   A list of all those responsible for the project. Animal handlers/trainers/suppliers are entitled to be listed for other than background work. Front credit is better than end credit, but it is virtually impossible for animal handlers to get. Credit in print work is listing you as supplying the animal or your animal's name.

**CUE**   A signal given to start or end any action. In the case of a human actor, that action can include a speech or line. The cue can be given via another actor's action or words, the director's signal or cue, or any other camera, light or equipment move. See also Appendix 2, Captain Haggerty's Key Light Cuing System.

**DAILIES**   Also known as rushes, they are generally reviewed by the director the day after shooting to see how he can improve the film. This is unedited film in rough form. Get to see the rushes. It will help you and your animal's performance immensely.

**DAY PLAYER**   An actor hired in film on a daily basis and paid by the day, as compared to an actor who is on a weekly basis and *may* make less per day. The weekly player is paid even if he does not work. These distinctions are important in quoting prices because they are the terms understood by the industry. This verbal shorthand not only communicates your idea but also can put more cash in your pocket.

**EDITORIAL**   A term used for work that is initiated by the publication. From your point of view, it generally refers to a photo session in which your animal is used at a lower, more favorable rate. If you give them a lower rate, insist on credit.

**END SLATE**   Instead of shooting at the head of the scene, the slate is shot at the end of the scene and held upside down to help identify it as an end slate. Also called a *tail slate.*

**EXTRAS**   Props that eat. Actors used as, and sometimes referred to as, atmosphere or background. Animal actors are used for this type of work, which is very easy. To save costs some production companies will attempt to hire actors who have the needed animal. Union rules require that a pittance be paid to the actor for supplying an animal. Human actors are sometimes so hungry that they will spend more money to bring the animal on the set than they are paid for the animal.

**FARGO, NORTH DAKOTA**   The sticks, the woods, Middle America. The primitive, albeit important netherworld between New York and Los Angeles. Sorry, North Dakota. I didn't make it up!

**FAVORED NATIONS**   A term used on a project in which all talent, including the star, has agreed to work for scale. It supposedly means that everyone is being treated the same. The only nation that is really being favored is the production company. If you are given this argument during negotiations, explain (a) there is no scale for animals and (b) animals are not "talent." Explain further you have no opportunity for residuals.

**FILM**   The preferred term, rather than movies. If you use the term "movies," you will seem less of a pro.

**FINAL CUT**   The absolute last word on how a film is to be edited. Nobody gets final cut. You will never get final cut, but if you are in some protracted negotiations, ask for final cut on the animal work. It will certainly get their attention.

**FLIES, FLY**   The area above a stage in which scenery, lights, weights and counterweights are suspended, stored or utilized. You want to keep your animals out of the flies because of the difficulty of retrieving them, particularly because of the tremendous height. A big problem with birds and primates. If you have a bird problem, you can wait until the set closes down. Shut off all the lights except the bright light in an anteroom. Birds will fly to the light, at which point you close the door behind them.

**FOG MACHINE**   Produces a fog that is offensive to many animals. Special considerations must be made when these machines are used. The fog can be particularly disconcerting to birds. Caution people before going on the set or stage about these potential problems. Different material for creating the smoke creates different problems, including slippery footing.

**FOLLOW SHOT**   A shot in which the camera follows a piece of moving action. This can be accomplished with a stationary camera, a traveling camera or a zoom lens.

**FOLLOW SPOT**   A strong spotlight with a great range that is used to follow an actor, animal or otherwise. This can be disconcerting to some animals and they should be desensitized to it.

**FOOD REWARD**   A technique used in training animals. It is similar and related to *baiting* and *luring* (see entries) but not identical.

**FRAME**   The perimeter of the photograph. In handling animals you must be aware of how the subject (animal) is framed so that you can be as close as possible without appearing within the frame yourself. Watch your shadow, too! It is perfectly permissible to ask how a shot is framed and even ask to look through the camera. Don't forget to ask. No one likes other people using their equipment without permission.

**GAFFER** The chief electrician. The person responsible for all lighting and power sources.

**GAFFER'S TAPE** More correctly, duct tape (for patching duct work). Extremely tough adhesive tape that is used extensively on film production. The whole world is held together by gaffer's tape.

**GAG** (1) A stunt performed by a stunt player; (2) any induced artificial effect, such as a gun shot wound, a burning building or an exploding car; (3) a photographic special effect.

**GELT** Yiddish. Money.

**GEVALT!** Yiddish. A cry for help. An all-purpose word for fear, apprehension, dissatisfaction, astonishment, amazement, horror. *"Gevalt!* All this work for so little *gelt."* Put an *Oi* before the *gevalt* and they'll know you speak the language.

**GONIF** Yiddish. Thief, dishonest person. "I'll be more than happy to give you a great animal for the job, but I can't afford to work for *gonifs."*

**GOY** Yiddish. A non-Jew. A gentile. The plural is *goyem.*

**GRIP** (1) Someone with a firm "grip" who is responsible for the moving and shifting of a wide variety of equipment. If you are on the set positioning your dog and a chair has to be moved two inches to the right, ask permission before you move it. Some grips are very possessive about their jobs, and union regulations prohibit you from moving the item. If you have gotten two or three yeas and no nays to "I can move it. Is it okay?" you can then move things as needed. A different day and a different job and you must go through the ritual again. If there are no carpenters on the set, that task would then fall to the grip. (2) Another term is a piece of equipment for mounting lights or cameras.

**HANDLER**  A person handling the animal, not necessarily its trainer. The words are generally used interchangeably, but there is a subtle (and important) difference. See *Wrangler* and *Trainer.*

**HANDLING**  The technique of producing the desired results with an animal needed for a performance. Best results are achieved by an excellent animal handler who is able to read the animal, give the commands, and supply the body english needed for the desired results. The effort is so fast and seamless that most people do not see or appreciate what is happening.

**HAZARI OR CHAZARI**  Yiddish. Pronounced with a hard, gutteral *ch* sound, not a soft *h* sound. Junk food. If they are feeding you in a less than satisfactory fashion, "We break our buns and these *gonifs* feed us *chazari.*"

**HOCK OR HAK**  Yiddish. To bargain. To hit. "Don't *hok* me on the price." Further development of complete Yiddish phrases are *Hak nit kain tshenik.* and *Hak nit in kop.* The first means "Don't bother me with your foolish yammering!" or, literally, "Don't bang on my tea kettle." The second, "Don't bang on my head." Remember that because Yiddish is the second language of showBiz, it is good to have a phrase or two standing in wait.

**HONDEL**  Yiddish. To bargain vigorously.

**HOOK**  (1) An interesting twist or ploy in a film's plot that makes the film; (2) a hook-shaped staff used to pull unsuccessful performers (or those exceeding their time allotment) off the stage; (3) a political or business connection who watches over you or makes sure you get the job. Similar terms would be "godfather," as in the film of the same name, or "rabbi," used incongruously by members of the New York City Police Department when it was dominated by the Irish with virtually no Jewish cops. The Yiddish word *mishpocheh* can be used in place of the word "hook." "He's my hook" becomes "He's *mishpocheh*."

**HOT SET**   A set in which everything (lighting, props, furniture, etc.) is in its exact position. It should not be disturbed or entered into, and I wouldn't even look at it to be sure.

**KEY LIGHT**   The main source of light. It is often used artistically to highlight an actor or a portion of the actor's face. Generally the light is placed high and to the side.

**KVELL**   Yiddish. To brag in glowing terms.

**LINE OF SIGHT**   An imaginary line. The actor is looking at something specific in his mind that deals with the action in the film. If you break (cross) the actor's line of sight, you break his concentration and can commit a tremendous blunder. Remember, you are handling an animal actor. Do not let anyone break your line of sight to your animal.

**LOCATION**   An actual location where the filming or taping takes place as opposed to a set.

**LOOP, LOOPING**   The worst four-letter word to a soundman. See *Automatic dialogue replacement.*

**LURING**   A technique for guiding an animal into a certain position or direction, usually, but not necessarily, with food.

**MACHER**   Yiddish, with a gutteral *ch*. As in, "big *macher*." One who does things, gets things done. The big *macher* is the one who makes decisions. The boss.

**MARK**   A spot an actor is to move to at the right instant, usually indicated by a piece of colored tape on the ground.

It is critical in the shooting of a film because of camera focus and lighting. It is difficult, at best, to have an animal hit the exact spot.

**MASTER SHOT** An overview of a scene, generally a wide shot in which all the action is shot. Close-ups are inserted in the editing to point up detail and add to the film.

**MAVIN** Yiddish. An expert. You are the animal *mavin*.

**MAZEL** Luck, as in good luck. More properly *mazel tov* means good luck.

**MCGUFFIN** The hook or trick that causes a film plot to move forward. A term devised by Alfred Hitchcock. Also a famous Bull Terrier immortalized in *McGuffin and Co.*

**MEGILLAH** Yiddish. The whole works. A lot. A long story. A lengthy list. An often-used phrase is "the whole *megillah*." As in, "You get me, you get my supertrained golden eagle, transportation, licenses, insurance—the whole *megillah* for that price!"

**MENSCH** Yiddish. A person, but more than that. A real person who is caring and considerate. A great compliment. "He's a real *mensch*."

**MESHUGGE** Yiddish. Crazy. A crazy man is *meshuggener* and a crazy woman *meshugeneh*.

**MISHPOCHE** Yiddish, with a gutteral *ch* sound. It means family, but in reality it is an extended family and can include everyone Jewish. If you are a gentile trying to get a film job for your pet and are introduced with the phrase "She's *mishpocheh*," you probably have the job. It means you are the closest of friends and anything you do for her you will be doing for me. Cherish that friendship. It is the highest of compliments.

**MITZVAH** Yiddish. (1) A blessing, a divine commandment; (2) A good deed. As in, "It's a *mitzvah* you hired my animal for this job. No other animal could do what you need here."

**MIX** Combining the various sounds such as dialogue, background sound, sound effects and music.

**MONOFILAMENT** A lightweight but extremely strong invisible material used by fishermen. In film it is used to move inanimate objects. It can also be used for controlling animals, but should only be used in a last-ditch effort to solve a control problem.

**MONTAGE** (1) A term used to mean editing. Basically it is the assembly of pieces of film to create moods, ideas, feelings, emotions or even a short story. Generally applied to an arty type of editing. When Rin-Tin-Tin attentively listened to instructions to get the cavalry because the bad men were coming through the pass to attack the farmers, the next piece of film shows Rinty running, and the next piece shows Rinty barking the message to the captain at the fort. All put together to create a story. (2) A collection of pictures/images within a frame.

**M.O.S.** This abbreviation means shooting a film or portion of a film without sound. It comes from the old-time film directors, who were often German, and said, "Mit out sound." Sound is generally added later. When working with animals this is great, because it makes your job easier. You can say and do anything to get your pet to perform.

**NO SEAM** A long roll of colored, seamless paper that is used for ground and backgrounds, generally in still shots. It creates the illusion of no horizon because there is no break between the ground and the background. It is continuous.

**POV, POINT OF VIEW** The direction that an actor is looking in from the camera's point of view. To illustrate an actor looking out a window at two kittens playing, the camera (from the kittens' POV) will view the actor standing in a window looking down, and then cut. The camera will be moved to the window to photograph the kittens so we know what the actor is looking at. The shot would be described as "from the actor's POV."

**PC, POLITICALLY CORRECT** An increasingly important concept in the handling and supplying of animals. It is difficult to say what is PC because it changes from day to day. If the animals are handled and trained in a better fashion than the human actors, it will be PC. Some people feel that using an animal on TV, in film or on the stage is exploitative and shouldn't be done. Such people, generally, have no understanding of animal behavior and they anthropomorphize.

**PREPRODUCTION** The preparations made prior to the shooting of the actual film or tape project. Preproduction and production functions overlap somewhat. Preproduction covers hiring talent, scheduling and budgeting. You may be contacted at this point to give a price quote (see Chapter 9).

**PRINT JOB** A photo session used for advertising or editorial purposes. A print job generally pays less than film, but you have a right to ask for a credit if you are working for less money.

**PRODUCTION** The physical work involved in shooting a film or tape project after the preproduction and before final editing. A project is "in production" when it is undergoing photography.

**PSA** A public service announcement, for which people will *hock* you on the price because it is for the benefit of the general public. Usually an ad agency will do a PSA free of charge, but all of the below-line personnel are paid union scale, including actors. Actors do not receive residuals for these PSAs.

**PUBLIC RELATIONS**   Good publicity. The use of animals can give a tremendous public relations boost to any production. Be prepared to give the production company as much assistance in this regard as they are willing to accept.

**PUTZ**   Yiddish, (1) Penis; (2) jerk, boob, simpleton, fool, yokel. See *Shmuck*.

**QUOTE**   As in, "What's your quote?" See *Rate*.

**RAG BUSINESS**   A somewhat derogatory term for the garment industry, in all its phases.

**RATE**   As in "What's your rate?" or what do you charge? Know the answer and don't be afraid to come up with a high figure. It actually means, What did you get on your last film? This is not to say that you can't work for less. Many stars will work for scale if the project is of interest to them. These are the real actors. Rates are quoted on a daily, three-day, weekly and complete-project basis. The higher up your remarkable Rhode Island Red rooster is in the show business pecking order, the longer the contract is for, even if it is for just a few days' work. You should know what category you are in. Most animals are quoted on a daily basis in film and TV and on an hourly basis for still shots or print. Quote a least a two-hour minimum.

**READ, READING**   (1) Reading an animal is the ability to know what is going on in its mind. This should be combined with judicious handling, which will produce the performance desired. (2) To be easily recognizable. A black-colored dog curled up in a corner sleeping with its head tucked under its tail might look like a blob. "It (the black dog) cannot be read." (3) To read lines off a script, as in (a) an audition; (b) a rehearsal; (c) to sell a script (generally for stage work). It is doubtful you would be called in for a reading, but you will be called in for an audition.

**RELEASE** (1) When a film is put into distribution; (2) form you will sign certifying that you are releasing all rights to the image of your animal's picture, performance, sounds, etc.

**RESIDUALS** Money paid for the rerunning of a commercial, film, etc. Animals are not normally paid residuals. The initial principle behind residuals is that every time an actor's face is shown, he is worth less. Animals are not readily identifiable, while certain breeds are identifiable. No one has a proprietary interest in a specific breed. That was the initial union argument for residuals, but collective bargaining has broadened the base and now puppeteers and stunt players are among those receiving residuals. In both these cases the actor is not recognizable. Clowns in proprietary makeup also receive residuals, although many of those receiving the residuals do not actually conform to the true definition of proprietary makeup.

**RUSHES** See *Dailies.*

**SCALE** Minimum acceptable salary for a union star. All rates go up from this figure. They cannot go down. As a matter of fact if there is an agent involved the minimum paid is "scale plus ten," which adds 10% for the agent because an agent's fee cannot invade the actor's scale rate according to union rules.

**SCRATCH TRACK** A sound recording made while the film is being shot, for use later when the sound is mixed. Also referred to as a *wild track.*

**SERIES** Feature-length films or TV shows with recurring characters in recurring situations. Series, today, generally refers to TV and is considered excellent, steady work. The Rambo, Rocky and James Bond films are also considered series.

**SET** An artificially constructed area that defines where the film, play or TV program is taking place. Generally sets are constructed indoors, although they may give the appearance of being indoors or out. In the early days of movie making, all sets were constructed outside to take advantage of the natural light. See *Location*.

**SHAGITZ** Yiddish. A male *goy*, or non-Jew.

**SHAYNA MADEL** Yiddish. Pretty girl. Also the name of a well-known play.

**SHIKSA** Yiddish. A female non-Jew.

**SHLEMIEL** Yiddish. A jerk, fool, boob, bumpkin. A nerd.

**SHLEP** Yiddish. To carry or drag, generally a heavy item. A *shlepper* is the type of inconsequential person you would hire to carry that heavy burden.

**SHLOCK** Yiddish. Shoddy, poor-quality, damaged merchandise.

**SHMALTZ** Yiddish. (1) Grease, fat, generally chicken fat; (2) corny, mushy, maudlin, overly romantic.

**SHMATTE** Yiddish. Literally, a rag. Now used to mean clothing, generally inexpensive. Sometimes incorrectly used to mean cheap goods.

**SHMEER** Yiddish. (1) To bribe; (2) to spread, as in, "Give me a bagel with a *shmeer*"; (3) an entire package, as in, "That's the price for the whole *shmeer!*"; (4) to hit or strike.

**SHMOOZE** Yiddish. Talking, chatting but in a friendly fashion to develop contacts with business or friends.

**SHMUCK** Yiddish. (1) The male member (extremely vulgar); (2) a jerk, idiot, boob; (3) an SOB. While offensive and vulgar, this word can be used in most show business settings with impunity. While it might be offensive if used on-camera at one of the Christian television networks, they won't know what it means anyhow. See *Putz*.

**SHNORRER** Yiddish. (1) A beggar, but a high-class, proud, educated, and intelligent beggar; (2) a chiseler, a cheapskate; (3) a compulsive and hard bargainer. When you are losing ground in the financial aspect of negotiations: "I want to do good work but you continually *hock* me. I can't afford to work for *shnorrers*."

**SHOT** Oftentimes used interchangeably with the word *take*. There is, however, a slight, subtle difference. A shot is what appears to be the single, uninterrupted operation of the camera that produces an uninterrupted action on the screen. In fact it *may* have been edited. A take is not edited, and it is what is shot in a continuous operation of the camera on the day of the shoot. A minor difference that is good to know, but no one will laugh at you if you use either term for the other.

**SHTARKER** Yiddish. Powerful man or strong-arm man. Used to refer to a heavy hitter, someone who is entitled to make more money in any deal because of his outstanding skills. As in, "This cat is a *shtarker*. You could pay more but couldn't get better." Said with a rising inflection on the end of the last sentence.

**SHTICK** Yiddish. The ultimate show business term meaning (1) a piece of business by a performer; (2) a piece. Pronounce that *sh*. The word is *not* a boomerang that doesn't come back. It is not a stick.

**SILENT BIT** A part in a film in which no lines are spoken. The rate of pay is higher than for an extra but lower than for a day player. The term is sometimes used for animals but really does not apply. It would mean the animal does nothing, but it must be featured in the foreground and do something as opposed to *background, atmosphere* or *extra*.

**SLATE** See *Clapper; End slate*.

**SMOKE**  See *Fog machine.*

**STAGE RIGHT OR LEFT**  Directions, meaning that you should move to the left or right, depending on which way the stage is facing.

**STORY BOARD**  A series of sketches (similar to a comic strip) in which all the shots are illustrated.

**STUDIO WORK**  A California term for supplying trained animals to studios for film and TV. See *Theatrical work.*

**TAIL SLATE**  See *End slate.*

**TAKE**  See *Shot.*

**TALENT**  Actors, even if they are not talented. While it also means your pet, it also encompasses extras and your pet. Animals can arbitrarily come under other categories, such as props. I much prefer the term *talent.*

**THEATRICAL WORK**  A New York term for supplying animals for film and TV production. See *Studio work.*

**TRACKING, TRAVELING, TRUCKING OR DOLLYING SHOT**  A shot in which the camera moves, sometimes on tracks, to follow an action, such as an animal running.

**TRAINER**  The person who actually trains the animal to do its assigned task. Training and handling duties may overlap, as when a trainer also handles the animal that he has trained. This is the highest accolade in the animal supplying fraternity. See *Handler* and *Wrangler.*

**TRAINING**  Teaching an animal to perform a certain exercise. See *Handling.*

**TSATSKE, TCHOTCHKE**  Yiddish. (1) Inexpensive toy; a bauble that looks small but can be expensive, a plaything; (2) a bimbo.

**TSURES** Yiddish. Trouble or aggravation. Singular is *tsurah*. "Sure I charge a few bucks more, but you won't have any *tsures* getting the shot."

**WEEKLY, WEEKLY PLAYER, WEEKLY RATE** Actors paid by the week are on a higher social stratum than those paid at a daily rate. Although the pay per day, at scale, is less than a daily rate, you are paid even if you are not required to work. Grab a weekly if it is offered to you.

**WILD TRACK** A recording made that is not in sync with the action in the scene. They will want some sounds of your animal for possible use in dubbing at a later date. Ask the sound man if he wants any wild track before you leave. During the lunch break is a good time to do the wild track. If you have it done before you are finished with the filming, you will not have to wait around to supply the sounds.

**WRANGLER** A term now applied to all animal handlers/ trainers. More properly, it refers to the people that wrangled horses in the heyday of Westerns.

**WRAP** The wonderful words you wait for all day. As in, "That's a wrap on the animal." They are not going to package your animal. Your job is finished and they are letting you go home.

**WRAP PARTY** The party given at the end of the film celebrating its completion. Often the animal handlers are forgotten about, so stay in touch with the production company to make sure you are invited. It is a great place to network and pass out your cards. If you are working for an animal agency, it is not right to hand out your own cards. Hand out the agency's cards. Do *not* bring your pet unless you clear it with the producer.

That's a wrap on this book!

# Index